Vegano Italiano

To all the women in my family
because they taught me so much

Vegano Italiano

150 VEGAN RECIPES FROM THE ITALIAN TABLE

ROSALBA GIOFFRÉ

THE COUNTRYMAN PRESS

A division of W. W. Norton & Company

Independent Publishers Since 1923

Acknowledgments

The author would like to thank the following people for supplying materials and props for the photographs:

Arti Meccaniche di Simone Innocenti

Ceramiche Virginia, Montespertoli (FI), Italy, www.virginiacasa.it

Pasquinucci, gifts for the home, Florence

Vulcania industria ceramica, Colle Val D'Elsa (SI), Italy, www.vulcaniaceramiche.it

She would also like to thank Pietro Rinaldi, fruit and vegetables, Florence.

Copyright © 2017, 2015 Giunti Editore S.p.A. Florence-Milan

Original title: *Vegano Italiano, Sapori vegani della nostra tradizione - Oltre 150 ricette*
Text by Rosalba Gioffré
Translation by Kosmos Srl 2017
Photographs by Lorenzo Borri
Graphic design and layout and editing of the Italian Edition:
Pier Paolo Puxeddu+Francesca Vitale studio associato
Illustrations by Pier Paolo Puxeddu
Illustration page 1 and 3 © Archivio Giunti/Pier Paolo Puxeddu

For information about permission to reproduce selections from this book, write to Permissions, The Countryman Press, 500 Fifth Avenue, New York, NY 10110

For information about special discounts for bulk purchases, please contact W. W. Norton Special Sales at specialsales@wwnorton.com or 800-233-4830

The Countryman Press
www.countrymanpress.com

A division of W. W. Norton & Company, Inc.
500 Fifth Avenue, New York, NY 10110
www.wwnorton.com

978-1-68268-054-4 (pbk.)

10 9 8 7 6 5 4 3 2 1

Contents

TRUE HOME COOKING

I became a vegan chef by chance. I ended up here quite by accident, without making any real decision and perhaps without even any particular vocation. Yet, just like many people these days, I am very conscious of, and interested in, the culture of veganism and its approach to food and nutrition.

I learned to cook from my mother and my grandmother, as well as from a host of aunts who were experts in improvising delicious lunches out of nothing.

I caught the bug from my vegan friends. I also do volunteer work, which means I often find myself—very willingly—cooking for vegan evenings. This brought vegan cooking to my attention and inspired me to experiment with appetizing, cruelty-free cuisine.

Like many others, I first got carried away with the latest trends and tried using techniques and ingredients from Asian and fusion cuisine. Then I started to wonder why I couldn't use my own way of cooking. Why did I have to ignore my culinary heritage, even if I was venturing into entirely new territory as a cook? Finally, I wondered what would happen to my culinary identity, all the cooking I had learned and practiced over the years, if I became vegan, and this frightened me a little bit.

I am a woman from Southern Italy. The memory of my family has been passed down through food; every recollection is tied to a *mangiata*, a hearty meal around a large table. Invariably, whenever we get together we talk about what we'd eaten or were about to eat.

I learned to cook from my mother and my grandmother, as well as from a host of aunts who were experts in improvising delicious lunches out of nothing, even with just the few vegetables that they could find in the garden. In reality, during the summer we always had plenty of vegetables, especially superb tomatoes and eggplants that we would use to make simple yet delicious dishes in no time at all. Meat was rarely on our table and butter was treated as something sinful. I remember that my mother would send me to buy half a stick from the grocer. This only happened when she was making pasta with butter, which, for us, was an extremely exotic and delicious dish. These were the basics

that I had to start with. At some point, I began to search through my memories and family recipes for vegan dinners and I discovered that I already had a very rich repertoire. I am able to draw inspiration from the things I learned to cook as a child, and explore infinite variations on the traditional cuisine of my native regions: Calabria, where I was born, and Tuscany, where I had a happy childhood even though I never felt completely at home.

With this in mind, I looked into the traditions of other Italian regions and found a plethora of recipes that are substantially vegan, or easily adaptable to vegan. Now that I've calmed down and realized that if I want to follow a vegan diet I don't have to completely change my habits in the kitchen, it almost comes naturally to cook without using animal products. It's a challenge and I really enjoy it. I get a lot of satisfaction from serving dishes to my enthusiastic dining companions.

So, consider this book an invitation toward a different approach to being vegan. These recipes are just examples. Do as I did. Start with the cooking style you know best and use ingredients that are familiar to you. You'll find out just how easy it is to make dishes that are delicious and vegan—without having to give up too much.

CRUELTY-FREE FOOD IS ALREADY ON OUR TABLES

It's true—I've tested it and put it into practice: You can be both vegan and a foodie. Choosing not to eat animal products doesn't mean having to entirely give up the food culture that you grew up with, nor does it mean having to get used to exotic ingredients. Tofu and seitan were introduced into the vegan diet so as to have some protein-rich substitutes similar to meat that are both satisfying to bite into and filling.

Using these ingredients can be very useful, especially during the transition from an omnivorous diet to a vegan one when it may be difficult to get used to cooking without meat, fish, or eggs. At the same time, eating too much tofu and seitan is in no way necessary and can even be harmful.

There is still fairly widespread belief that vegans live a life of deprivation—great suffering and horrible food. The exact opposite may be true because vegans, by carefully considering everything they introduce into their diet, end up consciously selecting only high-quality products and so may eat better than someone who eats everything. It's not a question of sacrificing; rather, replacing some foods that you don't want to eat anymore.

> In rural traditions and in Southern Italian cooking, vegetable dishes, especially those with potatoes, were often served as complete meals.

First and foremost, the key is to change your mind-set about what makes a meal. Vegetables are no longer a side dish or a diet food, but instead become the main course, the essential one. In hindsight, it has always been this way in Italy. In rural traditions and in Southern Italian cooking, vegetable dishes, especially those with potatoes, were often served as complete meals—often quite elaborately—when there really wasn't anything else to serve with them.

Legumes and grains are the cornerstone of a vegan diet. And eating them almost every day is really not that difficult in a country such as Italy where a good part of traditional recipes, especially in the north, are based on legumes and grains. There are as many pasta and bean recipes as there are Italian regions; there are spelt and barley soups to die for, not to mention chickpea *cacciucco* soup, baked chickpea pie, creamed fava beans, and other delectable legumes combined with vegetables. And then we have risotto: Many people nowadays, even those who are not vegan, make it with olive oil and vegetable stock and it offers endless possibilities for creating tasty recipes using the fantastic vegetables from our gardens.

I'll stop here, but I really could go on forever.

THE VEGAN REVOLUTION

The term *vegan* was coined by Donald Watson, an English craftsman from Yorkshire when, along with Elise Shrigley and four others, he founded the Vegan Society on a Sunday in November at the Attic Club in Holborn, London. It was 1944.

People become vegan for ethical reasons, or because they want to follow a healthy, balanced diet or even because the vegan concept is compatible with an ecological choice.

The word comes from *vegetarian*, without its central syllables, signifying that the new school of thought came from vegetarianism, itself established as an association in 1847. From an ethical point of view, there had been an unresolved debate for some time about the sustainability of eating eggs and dairy products.

Vegan, in short, also symbolically expresses the reduction of animal suffering by not using animal derivatives. Watson said in an interview, "The word 'vegan' was immediately accepted and became part of our language and is now found in almost every dictionary around the world."

In its more than 70 years of history, the Vegan Society—which had 25 members in the beginning—has become structured with an ever-growing membership. Many other associations have sprung up around the world: Their message has found a receptive audience across all sectors of society. More and more people are going vegan and their reasons are very personal and diverse: people become vegan for ethical reasons, or because they want to follow a healthy, balanced diet, or even because the vegan concept is compatible with an ecological choice and a fairer, more sustainable approach to food.

BEING VEGAN

I would like to quote the Articles of Association written when the Vegan Society became registered as a charity in 1979: "Veganism is a way of living, which seeks to exclude—as far as is possible and practicable—all forms of exploitation of, and cruelty to, animals for food, clothing or any other purpose; and by extension, promotes the development and use of animal-free alternatives for the benefit of humans, animals and the environment."

Being vegan is therefore primarily a lifestyle choice. Veganism is a worldview that is based on nonviolence and compassion toward all living beings, and in defense of animals as sentient beings. The vegan diet is based on a vegetarian diet, with the total exclusion of any ingredients of animal origin, for ethical reasons first and foremost. No meat and fish, of course. And no milk or cheese or eggs, and not even honey and royal jelly, because the production of these foods always involves the killing or the exploitation of animals.

It also follows that certain plant products, the production of which has an unacceptable cost for animals and the environment, are also excluded. The example that is often given is palm oil. Its cultivation leads to deforestation, wiping out animals and violating the rights of indigenous peoples. The intensive rearing of livestock is equally inadmissible, because it uses land that would otherwise be used for crop cultivation and produces highly pollutant materials.

IT'S NOT JUST ABOUT WHAT WE EAT

Vegans do not use any products that are in any way derived from the exploitation of animals. They don't wear wool or silk (only the legendary and elusive bourette silk, which is collected from the cocoons of butterflies after they have emerged), much less down jackets or fur coats. They do not wear leather shoes or carry leather bags, nor do they buy leather sofas. They do not use cosmetics, household products, or medications that have ingredients derived from animals or that have been tested on animals, even if they are so-called natural medicines, such as propolis. They don't eat truffles if they don't know who collected them, because the dog trained to search for them may have been mistreated. I almost forgot: They don't use wax candles, only paraffin ones.

IT'S EASIER BEING VEGAN IN MEDITERRANEAN COUNTRIES

We are the land of sun and lush fields, with vegetable gardens right outside our doors. Fresh fruits and vegetables are plentiful year-round.

The food pyramid of the Mediterranean diet largely reflects the basic foods of the vegan diet: first of all, fresh fruits and vegetables, then legumes and grains, dried fruits, nuts, seeds, oil, and water. We're lucky: Becoming a vegan in this part of the world may not be so complicated, except at the beginning when you have to change some ingrained habits.

We are the land of sun and lush fields, with vegetable gardens right outside our doors. Fresh fruits and vegetables are plentiful year-round, so much so that we export all over the world. The selection of local and seasonal ingredients in Italy is rich and varied. Just think about the many different culinary traditions of Southern Italy, prepared with fantastic vegetables in every way imaginable: countless classic recipes that represent the region's gastronomic heritage.

Just think about the exceptional olive oil that we are lucky enough to eat in or on our food without even thinking about it, because we're so used to having it in the kitchen. Think how easy it is to find genuine, high-quality, freshly picked, locally grown ingredients at our markets. Undoubtedly, we have an advantage over other countries where meat plays a larger role and the available vegetables are few and far between.

A LIFESTYLE THAT'S GOOD FOR THE BODY AND THE ENVIRONMENT

As the saying goes, your health is everything!

A well-balanced, plant-based diet—rich in nutrients and low in fat—that includes legumes and whole grains and is free from overly refined products or chemical additives or preservatives is extremely good for you. The vegan diet, thanks to the high intake of fresh produce that promotes the body's natural well-being, is commonly considered beneficial in counteracting the onset of degenerative and cardiovascular diseases, which can, in part, be caused by the saturated fat found in animal products. The important thing is maintaining a good amount of protein, which can be easily done by eating legumes, whole grains, nuts, and seeds. The latter contains the famous omega-3s, which we are unable to produce but that are essential for a number of important bodily functions. So, remember to add them to your salads or breakfast cereals. If the seeds are toasted, all the better—they are delicious.

Pay attention to vitamin B_{12}. It is not found anywhere in the plant world and it is essential for our health. Although our need for vitamin B_{12} is very low, a deficiency can actually pose a serious threat to the body, even resulting in nerve damage. So, if you stop eating meat, dairy products, and eggs, seek advice from a nutritionist and take supplements.

Keep in mind, if you are vegan, your "environmental footprint" will definitely be lower than that of someone who is omnivorous. I mentioned earlier that intensive livestock farming causes extensive environmental damage, harming agriculture and biodiversity. This type of farming uses vast water resources, while the animals produce a good deal of the greenhouse gases that cause global warming and an enormous amount of pollutants. The same applies to fish farms, which pollute the seas with toxic residues and threaten existing fish species. Undoubtedly, if you don't eat meat and fish, you are helping in some way to buck the trend and encourage a shift toward fairer and more sustainable food production.

> The vegan diet . . . is commonly considered beneficial in counteracting the onset of degenerative and cardiovascular diseases.

THE VEGAN PANTRY

First and foremost, Italian vegans use **local ingredients**, and if they happen to be organic and have zero food miles, that's even better. To add sweetness, vegans prefer **whole cane sugar or malt**, as sometimes animal derivatives are used to process refined sugar. Stabilizers of animal origin can also be found in yeast, so vegans buy certified yeast or use **cream of tartar**—which comes from grapes—mixed with baking soda. To thicken recipes or form a jelly for making Bavarian creams or puddings, they don't use animal-based gelatin, but **agar,** which is made from certain types of algae.

Then there are special products, which are included in the vegan diet to replace and integrate foods that are otherwise excluded. I believe that you can cook most vegan food with products sourced from Italy's own culinary traditions. However, for some recipes in this book, I have relied on plant-based milk and vegan butter because I really had no other choice. Let's take a quick look at the most important ones, so we can see how to use them.

Plant-Based Milk

Even though it contains none of the characteristics of animal milk, in terms of either nutritional value or flavor, plant-based milk is called milk as a matter of convention, as it is frequently used to replace milk in vegan recipes. However, it would be more appropriate to call it a plant-based liquid. In stores you will find vegan milks that have been industrially produced with various grains, legumes, and nuts. The most common is soy milk, as—in addition to its fairly neutral taste—the protein in soy, lecithin, is an emulsifier and can be a partial replacement for eggs. You can have some fun making plant-based milk at home—you can buy a machine for this very purpose—or why not try the recipes on page 25.

Vegan Cheese

Vegan cheese mainly consists of creams or soft compounds from nuts or legumes, and is used in cooking much the same way as cheese made from dairy would be. There are also harder vegan cheeses, which can be cut into slices. These are made with soy milk or yogurts, or legumes, combined with thickening agents, such as agar, spices, and different flavorings.

Nutritional Yeast

Made from dried brewer's yeast, nutritional yeast flakes taste similar to grated Parmesan and are often used in vegan diets as a replacement for cheese, or simply to add flavor to pasta, vegetables, and grains.

Seitan

Seitan is made from a gluten-rich flour (such as bread flour) that is soaked in water to remove the starch. It is then enclosed in cheesecloth and boiled in a broth flavored with soy sauce and algae. Seitan is often used as a replacement for meat in recipes, as it has a similar texture and a good protein content (however, in no way can it be considered an alternative from a nutritional viewpoint). Use it if you like it, but in moderation. It is concentrated gluten, so look out for intolerances.

Seitan is sold in blocks. You can cut it into cubes and sauté it with vegetables, make a ragout sauce or "meatballs," or cut it into thin slices and make scallops or cutlets. It has a rather distinctive taste, but it also absorbs flavor from seasonings and other ingredients.

Soy and Derivatives

We need to have a separate discussion when it comes to soy, given that it is often presented as a miracle ingredient due to its health benefits and the protection it offers against certain degenerative diseases. It is undoubtedly a good source of vegetable protein and iron, and is found in most vegan diets. That being said, recent studies have revealed the presence of natural toxins in soy, which are extremely harmful for the body. This is why nutritionists strongly advise against eating too much soy over extended periods of time. Products derived from fermented soy (miso, tamari, tempeh) can be used safely. Eat other soy products if you want to, but take care not to overdo it. There are also soy milks and yogurts, which you can make at home, as you will see in the upcoming chapter.

Tofu is made with soy milk that has been curdled and pressed in a process similar to cheese making. It is soft and silky, meaning you can use it to replace fresh cheese, in ravioli, for example. Alternatively, if you choose a creamier variety, you can use it to make desserts and creams—even savory ones. Since tofu has such a delicate taste and needs to be flavored, it is used mostly for texture.

Tempeh comes from yellow fermented soy and has a flavor that is somewhere between nuts and mushrooms. It is used frequently in Indonesian cuisine and has also been very successful in Italy as it has a nice texture and a strong flavor. It is often used in vegan cooking to make a ragout sauce, sometimes together with seitan. You can try adding it to the basic recipes that you will find later in this book.

BASIC RECIPES

These basic recipes are useful for making all of the other recipes that you will find in this book. I have also added two tomato sauces, which are essential for everyday family cooking. This section is ordered to broadly follow the pattern of a classic recipe book: basic stocks, sauces, and doughs, followed by some crucial tips for vegan cooking.

VEGETABLE STOCK

Makes about 1 quart stock

Clean and roughly chop all the vegetables and put them in a large stockpot, together with the herbs and, if you like, peppercorns. Add the water and salt. Bring the stock to a boil, then lower the heat and simmer until the vegetables are tender, about 1 hour. When ready, remove the vegetables with a slotted spoon, add more salt to taste, and strain using a colander.

Stock can be refrigerated for 2 to 3 days, after which it is best to freeze it.

2 celery stalks
1 large onion
1 large potato
1 medium tomato
1 bay leaf
1 sprig flat-leaf parsley
A few peppercorns (optional)
6 cups water
Salt

PESTO

Makes 4 servings

Wipe the basil with a cloth, but do not wash it (if the leaves are soaked, the pesto will become very dark), and put it into a blender or food processor together with the garlic, pine nuts, and a generous pinch of coarse salt. Blend these ingredients a little and then gradually add the olive oil, blending on a low speed until you get the right consistency.

Coarse salt absorbs more of the water from the basil leaves than fine salt, turning the sauce a lovely bright green.

¼ cup basil leaves
2 garlic cloves
2 teaspoons pine nuts
Coarse salt
⅓ cup plus 2 tablespoons
  extra-virgin olive oil

ITALIAN-STYLE SALSA VERDE

2 bunches flat-leaf parsley, chopped (about 4 cups)

1 garlic clove

2 tablespoons pickled capers

Coarse salt

6 tablespoons extra-virgin olive oil

Makes 4 servings

Put the parsley, garlic, capers, and a pinch of coarse salt into a blender or food processor. Blend these ingredients, gradually adding olive oil until you get an even sauce.

Add 2 tablespoons of vegan bread crumbs to get a thicker sauce.

MAYONNAISE

⅓ cup plus 2 tablespoons soy milk, chilled

⅔ cup sunflower oil

1 tablespoon fresh lemon juice

½ teaspoon mustard

A pinch of ground turmeric

Salt

Makes about 1 cup mayonnaise

Pour the chilled soy milk into the beaker of an immersion blender and blend on the lowest setting for about 2 minutes. Gradually add the oil and continue to blend at the same speed until you get a thick emulsion. Move the blender up and down in the mixture to whip some air into the mayonnaise. Add the lemon juice, mustard, turmeric, and salt to taste and continue to blend until the ingredients are well mixed, then refrigerate the mayonnaise in an airtight container.

Some brands of soy milk do not thicken when whipped, but I'd be at a loss to tell you which ones they are. You'll have to experiment. The good news is that, for the most part, vegan mayonnaise does not curdle!

BÉCHAMEL SAUCE

4 tablespoons (½ stick) vegan butter

½ cup all-purpose flour

2 cups soy or rice milk, warmed

Salt and freshly ground black pepper

A pinch of ground nutmeg

Makes 2 cups sauce

Melt the butter in a heavy-bottomed pan, then, using a whisk, incorporate the flour. Gradually add the warm milk (do not allow to boil—otherwise the flour will turn lumpy) while whisking constantly so that lumps don't form. Add salt and pepper to taste, plus the nutmeg, and continue to stir over low heat until the sauce starts to boil and coats a spoon.

TOMATO SAUCE

1 celery stalk

1 small carrot

1 medium red onion

1 garlic clove

2 pounds ripe beefsteak and plum tomatoes, seeded

6 to 7 tablespoons extra-virgin olive oil

A few basil leaves

Salt

Abundant sauce for 1 pound of pasta

Chop the celery, carrot, onion, garlic, and tomatoes and toss together in a large pot. Cook this mixture, covered, over low heat, for around 40 minutes, then strain through a sieve or blend it. If you are going to eat the sauce right away, put the pan back on the stove, add the olive oil, basil, and salt to taste and reduce the sauce until the oil rises to the top. Otherwise, refrigerate it in an airtight container for a few days or freeze it. Season it when you are going to use it, with even just some cold-pressed extra-virgin olive oil.

RAGOUT SAUCE

1 celery stalk

1 carrot

1 red onion

1 garlic clove

1 sprig flat-leaf parsley

6 to 7 tablespoons
extra-virgin olive oil

Salt

1 cup red wine

2 pounds ripe plum
tomatoes or canned
peeled tomatoes

Freshly ground
black pepper

Abundant sauce for 1 pound of pasta

Finely chop the celery, carrot, onion, garlic, and parsley with a kitchen knife or blender. Heat the olive oil in a deep pan over low heat, then add and sauté the vegetable mixture. Add a pinch of salt to soften the ingredients without over-cooking them. Add the wine and, when it has evaporated, add the tomatoes. Season with additional salt and pepper to taste, then simmer the ragout, covered, over low heat until the oil rises to the surface. This will take around 30 minutes.

PIZZA DOUGH

2½ cups all-purpose flour
(Italian "type 0")

A pinch of salt

1 ounce fresh cake yeast
(or 3 teaspoons
active dry yeast)

About 1 cup warm
water, plus more to
dissolve the yeast

Makes enough dough for one 15-by-10-inch pizza

Sift the flour together with the salt to form a well on your work surface. Dissolve the yeast in a little bit of warm, but not boiling, water—otherwise the yeast will lose its active qualities. Let's say it should be more than tepid, or else it will not rise perfectly. Pour the yeast mixture into the center of the flour mixture. Mix in the flour with the yeast, using your fingers, gradually adding up to 1 cup of warm water until you get a uniform dough. Knead it vigorously with your fists, adding a tiny amount of water if it gets too tough. You should get a soft, elastic dough that isn't too dry (it rises better). Set it aside in a warm place to rise, covered with a cotton cloth. The dough will be ready when it has doubled in size and you can press your finger into it without any resistance. This will take around half an hour to an hour (depending on the outside temperature and humidity).

FRESH PASTA

1⅔ cups durum wheat semolina

1⅔ cups all-purpose flour (Italian "type 0"), plus more for dusting

A pinch of salt

About 1 cup water

This recipe makes enough pasta for four or five people. It may seem like a lot of dough, but keep in mind that there will be some waste from the pasta-making process and that the pasta will reduce in weight as it dries.

Prepare the dough: Sift the two types of flour together with the salt on your work surface. Make a well, adding some—but not all—of the water to the dry ingredients. Work the flour into the water, mixing it in with your fingers and adding more water little by little until you have a uniform dough. Knead vigorously on a floured work surface until you get a smooth, elastic dough, then wrap it in a cotton cloth.

Prepare the pasta sheets: If you are going to roll the pasta by hand, you need to let it rest for at least an hour—otherwise it will be too elastic and it will not spread out. Alternatively, you can divide it into four or five pieces and start to roll it out with a pasta machine (see note). Be sure to flatten each piece well with your hands before putting it between the rollers of the pasta machine or it will break apart. If you are going to use a rolling pin instead of a pasta machine, press down the dough with your hands, then turn it out onto a well-floured surface, rolling back and forth from the center with the floured rolling pin. Turn it over every so often to get a round sheet. Wrap it around the rolling pin to turn it over and roll it out until you get the desired thickness. Keep the sheet covered with a damp cloth so that it does not dry out too much.

Cut the pasta: Flour the sheet of pasta well and then fold it into quarters (or roll it), then cut it with a flat-edged knife to make tagliolini, tagliatelle, or pappardelle. Unroll the pasta right away, cover it with a cotton cloth, and leave it to rest before cooking. If you want to make lasagna, simply cut the sheet into rectangles.

If you are using a pasta machine, follow the manufacturer's instructions. Usually the right thickness for tagliatelle is setting no. 5, whereas the setting for lasagna is no. 6.

PUFF PASTRY

3 cups all-purpose flour (Italian "type 0"), plus more for dusting

1¼ cups bread flour

A pinch of salt

About 1 cup cold water

1 pound (4 sticks) vegan olive oil or sunflower butter

Makes about 2⅔ pounds puff pastry

Prepare the dough: Sift the two flours together with the salt. On a work surface, knead 3 cups of the flour mixture together with enough water to get a soft, uniform dough. Wrap it in a floured cloth and set it aside to rest.

Prepare the butter block: Mix the butter with the remaining flour mixture on the work surface and mold it into a block. Wrap it in aluminum foil and refrigerate for half an hour. Then, take a lightly floured rolling pin and roll out the dough to form a square that is a little bit bigger than the butter block. Place the block in the center of the dough. If it has become too hard, soften it with your hands. The consistency must be similar to that of the dough, otherwise it will break it. Fold the four sides of the dough over it, then flatten it slightly with the rolling pin to get a rectangle. Refrigerate it, wrapped in aluminum foil, for 15 minutes.

Fold the dough: Roll out the dough until it is about ¼-inch thick. You should end up with a 24-by-8-inch rectangle. Fold it in on itself three times, then roll it out again in the opposite direction, fold it in three again, then refrigerate, covered, for another 15 minutes. Repeat this three more times. In the end you will have "turned" the pastry four times. Some people do six or even eight turns.

To get sweet puff pastry, add a pinch of sugar together with the salt to the water and flour mixture. If you're not using all of the pastry, I recommend splitting the dough into four or five pieces and freezing it.

PIECRUST

Makes one 9-inch piecrust

Sift the flour together with the salt onto a work surface and mix in the sugar. Place the cold butter in the center and mix it into the flour mixture, kneading with your fingertips, using quick movements so that it doesn't get too warm, until you have a mixture that resembles bread crumbs.

Mix in as much ice water as needed to bring the mixture together into a dough. Form into a ball and refrigerate it, wrapped in plastic wrap, for at least an hour. After an hour, you can roll it out with a lightly floured rolling pin for use, or it can be frozen.

To get a savory crust, just leave out the sugar.

Traditional Italian *pasta frolla* would use eggs. Some cooks replace them with a leavening agent of some sort, but I don't care for that.

- 2⅔ cups cake flour (Italian "type 00"), plus more for dusting
- A pinch of salt
- ⅓ cup sugar
- ¾ cup cold vegan sunflower oil butter
- 2 to 4 teaspoons ice water or chilled soy milk

SPONGE CAKE

Makes one 10-inch cake

Preheat the oven to 350°F. Oil and lightly flour a 10-inch cake pan.

Heat a little of the milk, transfer to a cup and dissolve the saffron in it, and set aside.

Sift the flour with the cornstarch, baking powder, and baking soda into a mixing bowl to form a well. Add the sunflower oil and sugar to the well and beat with a whisk. Add the remaining milk, a little at a time, whisking all the while so that no lumps form while incorporating all the flour. Add the saffron mixture and lemon zest and whisk for as long as it takes to get a smooth, uniform batter. Then, pour the batter into the prepared cake pan. Bake 25 to 30 minutes until the sponge cake is nicely risen with a golden crust.

When the time is up, try the spaghetti test: Insert a piece into the center of the cake and take it out immediately. If it's clean, you'll know that the sponge cake is baked.

Never open the oven door while the cake is rising.

- About 1¼ cups plant-based milk
- A pinch of saffron
- 1⅔ cups cake flour (Italian "type 00"), plus more for pan
- ¾ cup cornstarch
- 2 teaspoons baking powder
- ⅛ teaspoon baking soda
- ¼ cup sunflower oil, plus more for pan
- ½ cup sugar
- Zest of 1 lemon

2 cups soy or rice milk

Zest of 1 lemon

1 vanilla pod, cut in half lengthwise

¾ cup sugar

⅓ cup cornstarch

A pinch of salt

A pinch of ground turmeric

CUSTARD

Makes about 2 cups custard

Bring the soy milk to a boil in a small pot, together with the lemon zest and vanilla pod. In another pot, mix together the sugar, cornstarch, salt, and turmeric. Remove the zest and vanilla pod from the milk, then gradually add the milk to the dry ingredients, beating the mixture with a whisk to stop lumps from forming. Place over low heat and, using a wooden spoon, stir until the cream thickens. Transfer the cream to a bowl and let it cool, covered by plastic wrap.

EGG SUBSTITUTIONS

Eggs are used in recipes to bind the ingredients together or to help a dough or mixture to rise. Generally speaking, when a lot of eggs are called for (let's say more than three), they are used as a leavening agent. Taking this into consideration, we can replace them with vegan ingredients that have a similar effect.

When egg is needed as a binding agent, you can replace it with any of the following:

- 2 tablespoons potato starch, cornstarch, rice flour, or chickpea flour (plus 2 tablespoons of water)
- mashed potatoes (savory recipes)
- cooked rice (savory recipes)
- ½ ripe banana (sweet recipes)
- ¼ grated apple (sweet recipes)
- ¼ soy yogurt (binding and leavening agent)

When egg is used as a leavening agent, you can replace it with any of the following:

- 1 tablespoon cider vinegar
- 2 tablespoons powdered soy milk diluted in the same amount of water
- 1 teaspoon baking powder plus ½ tablespoon baking soda.

Every time you make a substitution for a recipe you should think carefully in order to respect the balance of the ingredients.

PLANT MILKS

SOY MILK

For about 4 cups milk

2/3 cup yellow soybeans

4 cups water

A pinch of salt

Cover the soybeans with water in a bowl and allow to soak for 24 hours, then rinse them and place them in a pot with the 4 cups of water and salt and cook for about 20 minutes. Remove the skins that eventually rise to the top, using a slotted spoon, and then blend everything that's left. Cover a fine-mesh strainer with cheesecloth and place it over a mixing bowl. Gradually pour the soy mixture through the cloth to filter it, then wring out the cloth with your hands if it's not too hot. Pour the soy milk into a glass bottle and refrigerate. It will keep for 3 to 4 days. You can use the soy paste left on the cheesecloth to make "meatballs" or you can even add it to bread dough.

You can make rice, barley, and oat milk using the same technique. It is also possible to use a centrifugal juicer: After cooking, drain the beans, leave them to cool, and spin them together with 4 cups of water in the juicer.

ALMOND MILK

For 4 cups milk

2 cups blanched almonds

Water

Cover the almonds with water and leave to soak in a bowl and allow to soak for an hour. Afterward, put them in a blender along with their soaking liquid and blend the almonds to a pulp on the highest speed setting. Add as much water as needed to get 4 cups of liquid and blend again until the almonds are mashed. Filter through a fine strainer covered with cheesecloth, then pour the almond milk into a glass bottle and refrigerate. It will keep for 2 to 3 days. Don't throw away the almond paste. Mix it into praline or cookie doughs.

You can add a sweetener (sugar, malt syrup, agave nectar) when you blend the almonds.

VEGAN CHEESES

ALMOND CHEESE

4 cups almond milk

A pinch of salt

5 tablespoons cider vinegar or lemon juice

Bring the almond milk to a boil in a small pot, add the salt and vinegar, then remove from the heat and set aside to cool. Let it rest in the refrigerator for at least an hour, then strain the cheese curds that will have formed, using a fine-mesh strainer, and refrigerate in a bowl. After an hour, the cheese should have solidified; otherwise, wait a little longer and then turn it over onto a plate and serve. It will keep in the refrigerator for 6 to 7 days.

1⅓ cups raw cashews

1 teaspoon nutritional yeast flakes

2 tablespoons cider vinegar

A pinch of salt

Soy milk

CASHEW CHEESE

Place the cashews in a bowl, cover them with water, and allow them to soak overnight. Strain them and place them in the blender together with the yeast flakes, vinegar, and salt, and blend until you get a nice, smooth cream. Add soy milk until you get a creamy, not too hard consistency. Place the cream into a mold and allow it to set in the refrigerator for a few hours. You can flavor the cashew cheese however you like—with freshly chopped herbs, chili powder, or tahini. You can also make an outstanding raw almond cheese using the same method.

SEASONAL RECIPES

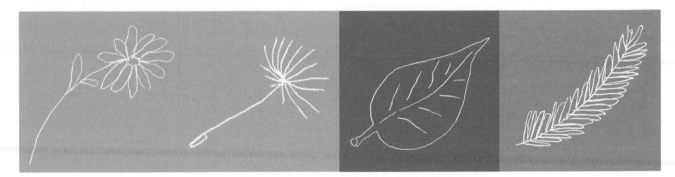

Vegetable Preparation

You'll notice that I never mention washing or cleaning the vegetables in the recipes, except when you need to follow a special technique, such as for the Giudia artichokes. I think that's a given. There's no need to repeat that vegetables, even organic ones or the ones you grow yourself in your garden, should always be cleaned and—more important—washed well.

I should say, however, that according to the best principles of vegan cooking, vegetables should be cleaned as little as possible, as all the nutrients and beneficial substances are found in the external layers. The vegan chef throws away the absolute minimum when it comes to salads and leafy vegetables, and tries to avoid peeling vegetables, or to use the skins or the outer leaves that have been removed in other recipes and dishes

Cooking Pasta and Rice

Cooking times will vary for fresh pasta and dry pasta and depending on the shape of each pasta. Various types of rice will also have different cooking times. Unless the recipe provides specific instructions, follow the cooking times indicated on the package.

Quantities

The quantities given in this book are just a guide. In other words, they are not exact down to the very last ounce. I have partially followed the tradition of home cooking, where you can vary the quantities a little without ruining the outcome of the recipe, and every so often you can estimate without worrying about it. In some recipes you might even find the quantities a little generous.

For the rest, as Italian grandmothers would say, where there are four at the table, there can also be five, and it is always better to cook a little extra, instead of not enough. What's more, all these dishes are delicious the day after, too, if there happen to be leftovers . . .

APPETIZERS

Spring Crostini, 30

with Braised Fava Beans
with Sautéed Asparagus
with Mint-Flavored Peas and Carrots

Spicy Vegetable Fritters, 32

Erbazzone/Chard Pie, 33

Fried Flowers, 34

Sicilian Arancini, 35

Piedmont Garden Salad, 36

Artichoke Salad, 38

Salad with Strawberries, 39

FIRST COURSES

Spring Minestrone, 40

Risi e Bisi/Rice and Peas, 41

Bucatini and Fava Beans, 42

Cicerbita Greens and Dandelion Soup, 44

Tagliatelle with Chickpeas, 45

Trenette Pasta with Pesto, 46

Spaghetti with Wild Asparagus, 47

Maccheroncini Pasta with
Puntarelle Greens, 48

Lasagna with Asparagus, 49

Spring Risotto, 50

SPRING

MAIN COURSES

Giudia Artichokes, 52

Fennel in Tomato Sauce, 53

Pie of Greens, 54

Onion and Olive Frittata, 55

Vegetable and Potato Sauté, 56

Roman Vegetable Sauté, 58

Breaded and Fried Asparagus, 59

Green Beans in Tomato Sauce, 60

Baked Swiss Chard, 61

DESSERTS

Chocolate Chantilly with
Strawberries, 62

Cherry Strudel, 64

Biancomangiare/Blancmange, 65

Sweet Rice Fritters, 66

Panna Cotta, 67

SPRING CROSTINI

This is the season when the great vegetable feast begins. Mother Nature awakens from her slumber and our gardens flourish with early fruits and vegetables, with wild herbs springing up everywhere. I'm lucky enough to have a little vegetable garden of my own. It's a flowerbed really. I only grow a few things because, although I come from a farming family, hoeing abilities were more or less lost after my mother and her sisters' generation. Nonetheless, my greens are the most delicate and tasty ones that I have ever eaten and my peas (there aren't many to tell the truth) are the sweetest—so much so that we always end up eating them raw. I'm late every year when it comes to fava beans—I never manage to plant them at the right time—but luckily, my aunts send me theirs from Southern Italy, and they are perfect for the following recipe.

CROSTINI WITH BRAISED FAVA BEANS

1⅓ cups fresh fava beans, shelled

1 sweet red onion, sliced

1 tablespoon tomato paste

Extra-virgin olive oil

Salt

Dried chili pepper, finely chopped, to taste

4 slices vegan whole-grain bread, toasted

Remove the eyes of the beans and notch them with your fingernail, otherwise the skin will split and separate from the pulp. Put them in a small or medium pot with the onion, tomato paste, olive oil, salt, and chili pepper. Add an inch of water and cook, covered, over low heat, for about 30 minutes, until they are tender. Spread them on the toast and serve hot, with some of their sauce drizzled on top.

CROSTINI WITH SAUTÉED ASPARAGUS

1 bunch asparagus

1 spring onion, sliced

Extra-virgin olive oil

Salt and freshly ground black pepper

4 slices vegan rustic bread, toasted

To remove the woody end, gently bend each asparagus spear until it snaps naturally. Cut the asparagus into 1-inch pieces and cut the tips in half lengthwise. Put them in a medium skillet with the sliced spring onion, olive oil, salt and pepper to taste, and a drop of water. Cook them, uncovered, over high heat until they are al dente. Spread them on the toast and finish with a good sprinkling of pepper.

CROSTINI WITH MINT-FLAVORED PEAS AND CARROTS

1⅓ cups fresh peas, shelled

2 baby carrots, diced

Extra-virgin olive oil

1 garlic clove (one half for each vegetable)

Leaves from 1 mint sprig

Salt

4 slices vegan whole-grain bread, toasted

Freshly ground black pepper

Cook the peas and carrots separately in a small pot with some oil, garlic, a few mint leaves, and a little bit of water. Add salt to the carrots right away, but only add to the peas once they are almost cooked, otherwise they'll become tough. Remove the garlic and lightly mash the peas with a fork, then spread them over the slices of toast. Place the carrots on top, then garnish with a few mint leaves and pepper to taste.

SPICY VEGETABLE FRITTERS

These are as easy as can be. Just cut the vegetables into thin slices, sticks, or cubes, put them in a bowl, and then throw in enough flour and water to create a light batter. Salt, some herbs . . . and then spoon these into a deep pan with 2 inches of almost, but not quite, boiling oil. Housewives used to make these to use up leftover, uncooked vegetables, sometimes without even peeling them. I always make them when I have leftover vegetables, both raw and cooked, even to make just a few fritters that my children can devour while they are waiting to eat—usually they disappear while I am frying them!

FOR 4 PEOPLE

1 bunch Swiss chard

½ garlic clove, chopped

1 sprig flat-leaf parsley, chopped

Crushed dried chili pepper, to taste

1 cup all-purpose flour

Salt

Cold water

Peanut oil for frying

Remove the center stems of the chard leaves, blanch the chard for a few minutes in a pot of salted, boiling water, then remove the leaves and squeeze out the water.

Place the chard, garlic, and parsley together in a bowl with some chili pepper.

Add the flour and a pinch of salt, then stir in as much water as is needed to bind all the ingredients together to get a rather liquid mixture.

Heat a generous amount of oil in a deep skillet, then add the mixture to the hot oil by the spoonful.

Remove the fritters with a slotted spoon when they turn golden and place them on paper towels to absorb the excess oil.

Serve piping hot with a sprinkling of salt.

Why not try to use the same method but with raw artichoke stems or finely chopped pea pods instead?

ERBAZZONE/ CHARD PIE

I've chosen this traditional savory pie from the culinary repertoire of Reggio Emilia to serve as an example and inspiration for all the savory pies imaginable, making use of the fantastic spring vegetables. The distinctive feature of the *erbazzone* pie, known as *scarpazzone* (*scarpa*—"shoe" in Italian—is meant to be the chard) in the Emilian dialect, is that it does not include ricotta or any other cheese. So, without the lard that they add to everything around those parts, this pie is vegan. Actually, it's supervegan. Its matzo crust may suggest some link with Jewish cooking.

Preheat the oven to 350°F. Sift the flour with a pinch of salt onto a work surface, stir in the oil, and then pour in the water, little by little, until you get a rather dense mixture. Knead it vigorously with your hands, until the dough is even and elastic. Place the dough in a bowl, cover it with plastic wrap, and leave it to rest for around an hour.

Blanch the chard in a large pot of salted, boiling water, drain it, then squeeze out any excess water and shred it.

Heat a little oil in a medium skillet. Sauté the onion and parsley in the oil. Add the chard and salt and pepper to taste and cook it— taking care to stir it every so often—until well seasoned. This will take around 10 minutes.

Divide the dough into two pieces, one slightly larger than the other. Roll out the larger piece with a rolling pin on a floured work surface to cover the bottom and edges of a 10-inch round baking pan. Spread the chard over it evenly.

Roll out and cut a disk from the remaining pastry, place it over the chard and seal the edges of the two pieces of dough with your hands, pulling the top piece over the other to create an edge.

Pierce the top of the pie with a fork and bake in the oven for around 35 minutes.

2½ cups all-purpose flour, plus more for dusting

Salt

Extra-virgin olive oil

Cold water

2 pounds Swiss chard

½ onion, diced

1 bunch flat-leaf parsley, chopped

Freshly ground black pepper

FOR 4 PEOPLE

Of course, you can also go against tradition and change the filling by using another type of vegetable, as long as it has a strong taste and a certain consistency (for example, peas, which would spill out all over the place as they are small and round, don't work well).

FRIED FLOWERS

I can't help but laugh whenever I think about the times I wanted to make fried zucchini flowers for my American friend and he would say, quite pointedly, in English: "I don't eat flowers." We Italians, on the other hand, do eat flowers and with great gusto! My grandmother used to add elderflowers—she called them May flowers—to her bread dough, with a bit of oil. The result was a kind of aromatic focaccia bread that went into the wood-burning oven when there was still a flame. Elderflowers added to a batter and then fried is something altogether special. Acacia flowers are also delicious. Be sure to pick them far from any source of pollution—it is better not having to wash them, as they will lose a lot of their scent.

Make a runny batter in a bowl with the flour, cold water, and a pinch of salt. Thoroughly beat it with a whisk to prevent lumps from forming, then leave it to rest in the refrigerator for around half an hour.

Heat a generous amount of oil in a deep skillet. You'll know the oil is ready when it starts to bubble: throw a drop of batter in the oil, if it floats to the top immediately, the oil is at the right temperature. Toss the flowers into the batter one by one, then fry them, a few at a time, in the hot oil.

Remove the flowers with a skimmer when they are nicely golden, then leave them to dry on paper towels.

Serve piping hot with a sprinkling of salt.

These flowers are also delicious with a dusting of sugar on top, thanks to their delicate and sweetly aromatic flavor.
If you would rather use petal flowers (such as nasturtium or pansy), mix them in a batter that is a little firmer and then toss them into the boiling oil by the spoonful. You will get wonderful fritters. You might also try using fresh borage flowers (starflower) or fennel tufts.

¾ cup all-purpose flour

Cold water

Salt

4 elderflower blossoms

4 bunches acacia flowers

Peanut oil, for frying

FOR 4 PEOPLE

SICILIAN ARANCINI

You would be right in thinking that these are substantial as starters—an arancino is practically a meal in itself. And of course, rice gives you that lovely feeling of being full right away. When I was young my aunts would make pear-shaped ones. When I was a little older, my cousins and I would go on raids in the afternoon—atop a Vespa—looking for the best rice balls in the local bars. And they were so delicious because they, too, were homemade and fried in olive oil.

FOR 4 PEOPLE

A pinch of saffron

2½ cups Arborio rice

½ onion, diced

Olive or peanut oil, for frying

1⅓ cups peas, shelled

1 cup tomato sauce

Salt and freshly ground
    black pepper

1⅓ cups all-purpose flour

About 1¼ cups cold water

Vegan bread crumbs

Dissolve the saffron in a cup of very little water and set aside.

Cook the rice in a large pot of salted boiling water, 15 to 20 minutes, or acording to package directions. Drain the rice, mix in the saffron mixture, and leave to cool.

Sauté the onion, without browning it, in a medium skillet with a little oil. Then add the peas and tomato sauce. Season with salt and pepper to taste and reduce on low heat for around 15 minutes.

Make a batter in a bowl with the flour, cold water, and a pinch of salt.

Put two spoonfuls of rice into the palm of your hand, flattening it into the shape of a bowl, and place just over 1 teaspoon of the pea sauce in the center. Close it with more rice and create the classic, round shape for the rice ball.

Roll each rice ball in the batter and then the bread crumbs, pressing them down firmly, then refrigerate the balls for about an hour.

Heat enough oil in a deep skillet to cover the rice balls almost completely. Fry the rice balls in the hot oil. Remove them with a skimmer when they are nicely golden and leave them to dry on paper towels.

When it comes to frying, you are better off using a small pan with high edges so that you can cook a few rice balls at a time in a lot of oil.
If you would like to try a different version, add ⅔ cup of mushrooms to the pea sauce.
In the spring we have delicious prugnoli mushrooms in Italy; however, button mushrooms and dried mushrooms are fine, too.

PIEDMONT GARDEN SALAD

In classic culinary language, *giardinetto*—"little garden"—is a composition of similar ingredients, yet with different colors, which manages to recall the image of a colorful garden. When it comes to putting this salad together, the idea really is all about bringing the fullness of the colors of a spring garden to mind. Marinated vegetables and fresh, crunchy salad have to be arranged on the plate with extreme care and with a touch of flair. This is a collection of extremely simple flavors, created as a side dish, yet it is also perfect as an appetizer.

FOR 4 PEOPLE

1 pound new potatoes

4 baby carrots

2 lettuce hearts, quartered

2 bunches radish, sliced

8 marinated artichoke hearts

Extra-virgin olive oil

Fresh lemon juice

Salt and freshly ground
    black pepper

Boil the potatoes in a medium to large pot with their skins still on, or peel them and steam them. Cook the carrots in the same way, after peeling them gently. If both the carrots and potatoes are very small, leave them whole; otherwise cut the potatoes in half and cut the carrots lengthwise.

Place the lettuce hearts on a plate and decorate by alternating the other vegetables.

Whisk the oil with the lemon juice, salt, and pepper to taste, until you get a nice emulsion.

Dress the garden salad with this emulsion and serve.

If you want a more fragrant salad, just add some chopped chives and parsley.

ARTICHOKE SALAD

Castraure are extremely tender baby artichokes. They are the buds that grow at the top of the plant and are cut around April, so as to encourage the other artichokes to grow underneath. Castraure are Venetian specialties: if we want to be very exact, the best come from Sant'Erasmo Island. These baby artichokes are cooked in a million different ways in Venice, yet it is best to eat them raw with a light dressing, because they are so tender and sweet.

FOR 4 PEOPLE

8 castraure artichokes

Fresh lemon juice

Salt and freshly ground black pepper

Extra-virgin olive oil

Clean the artichokes as little as possible, then put them in a bowl and cover with water and lemon juice to stop them from turning brown.

Dry them thoroughly and, using a sharp knife, cut them into very thin slices and put them into a salad bowl.

Season with salt and pepper to taste, a drizzle of oil, and nothing else.

Serve them with some thinly sliced toast (but this is not essential). You may not feel like eating bread with raw artichokes, and maybe you won't even like them with wine, due to the high tannin levels in the artichoke.

The Venetians also cook castraure *in tecia*—"in a pan"— with some fried onion and wedges of fennel.

SALAD WITH STRAWBERRIES

Spring is the best time of the year to indulge your craving for fresh, healthy food, and to try tender, crunchy salads with fresh leaves. When it comes to lettuce, I love early Canasta and Pesciatina lettuces. That's why, come spring, I manage to dig out a small patch—with much effort—in my very own vegetable garden, in which I place my favorite freshly sprouted salad plants. I cut them every day, not letting them grow too much, and then I plant new ones gradually as I cut. Sometimes I add other vegetables to my salad bowl and I have even started adding in some fruit and—every so often—toasted seeds. This is how I discovered that strawberries are fantastic in salads, especially when served at the beginning of a meal.

Remove the Canasta and Pesciatina leaves, clean the other greens, and then wash them all together and dry thoroughly. Peel and grate the carrots, then clean the strawberries quickly under running water and dry, hull, and slice them.

Tear the salad leaves with your hands and place in a nice salad bowl, together with the carrots and strawberries.

Dress the salad with oil and salt to taste just before serving and, if no one is looking, mix the salad with your hands—it's the best way to work the dressing into the salad.

Have a pepper grinder on hand as some people may wish to use it.

It almost seems trivial to say, but since there are strawberries, balsamic vinegar goes great with them.

2 small heads Canasta lettuce (or Bibb lettuce)

2 heads Pesciatina lettuce (or Boston lettuce)

1 bunch arugula

1 bunch oak leaf lettuce leaves

1 handful mâche

2 baby carrots

1 pint strawberries

Extra-virgin olive oil

Salt

Freshly ground black pepper

FOR 4 PEOPLE

SPRING MINESTRONE

There's no particular recipe. Minestrone is a jumble of flavors that change with the vegetables used, which are always different depending on the different places in Italy and the time of year. Once upon a time it was made with whatever was in the vegetable garden, the seasonal vegetables and herbs that were around, and a few seasonings. Today the prevailing rule is that the more vegetables you add, the more flavor it will have. The most famous minestrone soup would be the Milan recipe, which even bears the mark of authenticity, the Denominazione Comunale, a quality-assurance label certifying that it is a traditional recipe. This is an extremely hearty, dense soup that also contains rice. It has nothing in common with the recipe that I'm about to show you, which—according to my family's traditions—is a light dish with not too much seasoning, and is flavorful because of all the spring vegetables that are in it.

FOR 4 PEOPLE

1 spring onion

2 baby carrots

1 celery stalk

1 bunch thin asparagus

1 bunch Swiss chard

2 potatoes

Extra-virgin olive oil

1 cup fresh peas, shelled

1 cup fresh fava beans, shelled

Fresh thyme, rosemary, and marjoram, chopped

About 4 cups water

Salt

Slice the spring onion, including the green tops, cut the carrots into rounds and the celery into small pieces, and set aside.

Cut the asparagus into small pieces, removing the tough ends; cut the Swiss chard into uneven strips; and dice the potatoes.

Cover the bottom of a large pot with oil, then toss in the spring onion and heat it a little. Add all the vegetables, including the peas, fava beans, and herbs.

Lightly sauté the vegetables, stirring often, then add about 4 cups of water and bring to boil.

Season with salt and cook, covered, over low heat until the vegetables have cooked, but are still whole, for around 30 minutes.

Serve the Spring Minestrone with a drizzle of oil on top.

You can also make it heartier with some pasta: about ½ cup of mafaldine (ribbon-shaped pasta) per person, drained when it is very al dente and then added to the soup to finish cooking. Add some water from the pasta to make sure the soup doesn't become too dense.

RISI E BISI/RICE AND PEAS

I've always loved the Venetian dialect. I used to watch the comedic works of Carlo Osvaldo Goldoni, the famous playwright from the Republic of Venice, with my mom on television in the sixties, and the Venetian way of speaking would always fill me with glee. Saying *risi e bisi*—"rice and peas" in Venetian—instead of *riso e piselli*—"rice and peas" in Italian—sounds like something else altogether. It's an entirely different kettle of fish. Giuseppe Maffioli, the famous connoisseur of Venetian cuisine, tells us that it was a dish served to the doge, the leader of Venice, and was traditionally made on the feast day of Saint Mark. It spread to the rest of the Serenissima Republic and, from there, to all the cities of the eastern Adriatic, Greece, and Turkey. Vialone Nano rice from Grumolo delle Abbadesse was always used and the peas were the extremely sweet ones grown in Peseggia, where a bisi festival is held every year.

Heat a little oil in a large pot. Briefly sauté the garlic and onion with the peas in the oil. Let them develop some flavor, then add the rice and cover with the stock.

Bring it to boil and then finish cooking, covered, over a low heat, for around 20 minutes. Make sure that you season with salt and pepper to taste only at the end, otherwise the peas will harden.

The risi e bisi should now be somewhere between a risotto and a soup.

Serve with some parsley on top.

Maffioli suggests making a stock to cook the rice from the pea pods. You need to make sure that they are very tender and, after they are cooked, you should work them through a sieve to make a sort of puree to mix in with the stock.

Extra-virgin olive oil

½ garlic clove, chopped

1 white onion, diced

2 pounds peas, shelled

1½ cups Vialone Nano or Carnaroli rice

4 cups vegetable stock (page 17)

Salt and freshly ground black pepper

1 sprig flat-leaf parsley, chopped

FOR 4 PEOPLE

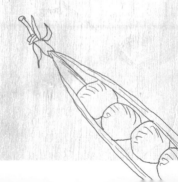

BUCATINI AND FAVA BEANS

I like to make this dish to shock my Florentine friends who are still convinced that fava beans should only be eaten raw with pecorino, practically as soon as they have formed. Where I come from, however, we let them grow a bit bigger, so that they develop a stronger flavor and hold up better when cooked. Pasta and fava beans is to die for when you use bucatini pasta that has been broken in two. However, I have—on occasion—used short pasta, such as mafaldine, especially when I'm making it for a lot of people, and it's not bad. When you shell the fava beans, make sure that you remove the eyes and notch them with your fingernail. If they happen to be really big, remove the skin, too. Your effort will be rewarded by a pasta and fava beans dish that is simply . . . favulous!

Place the fava beans with the onion, a bit of chili pepper, the tomatoes, and 4 to 5 tablespoons of oil in a large pot, then fill it up halfway with water. Leave it to cook over low heat until the fava beans are tender.

Boil the bucatini until they are half cooked, drain, and add to the pot with the fava beans to finish cooking. Season with salt and pepper to taste and, if necessary, add some hot water.

The pasta with the fava beans should be *all'onda*: in other words, creamy and not too reduced.

It is also delicious cold. All you have to do is drizzle some oil on it to soften it a little since it hardens quite a bit when it cools.

1 pound fava beans, shelled

1 large, sweet red onion, sliced

Dried chili pepper, finely chopped, to taste

2 plum tomatoes, finely diced

Extra-virgin olive oil

½ pound bucatini pasta, broken in two

Salt and freshly ground black pepper

FOR 4 PEOPLE

CICERBITA GREENS AND DANDELION SOUP

During the spring my mother used to take us out into the fields to pick wild greens. The ones that we came across the most were cicerbita (wild chicory, or sow thistle) and dandelion—which my mom didn't like very much. I, on the other hand, was crazy about dandelions, especially the fluffy head of seeds that I would always pick just to be able to blow and make a wish, despite the legend that says that they have an embarrassing effect on anyone who gets too close (another name for dandelions in Italian is *piscialletto*—"bed wetter"). Dandelions are a kind of cure-all for the liver: diuretic, purifying, and stimulating for the appetite, yet they are so bitter! Cicerbita, on the other hand, is sweet, deliciously crunchy, and just a little prickly. That is why these two wild herbs seem like a match made in heaven and why I have thrown them in the pot with some potatoes, to give the cream a bit of thickness.

FOR 4 PEOPLE

1 onion, sliced

Around 3 cups chopped dandelion and cicerbita or chicory leaves

2 cups diced potato

Extra-virgin olive oil

Salt

Vegan croutons, for serving

Freshly ground black pepper

Put the onion, greens, and potato into a medium to large pot with a little oil. Leave it for a few minutes to develop some flavor, then cover with boiling water and season with salt.

Cook over low heat until the potatoes are nearly overcooked, around 15 minutes, then blend it all with an immersion blender.

Serve the soup garnished with a few croutons and a sprinkle of pepper. You can even decorate the plates with some dandelion flowers, if you like.

My mom would sear the wild greens and then finish cooking them with white beans in a kind of soup, or she would sauté them in a pan with garlic, oil, and dried chili pepper.

TAGLIATELLE WITH CHICKPEAS

I always combine legumes with vegetables that are a little bitter, such as *barba di frate*—literally "monk's beard" in Italian—otherwise known as opposite-leaved saltwort, a succulent shrub that grows in the Mediterranean. I go crazy for this food pairing, especially with fresh, homemade pasta. Chickpeas don't generally fall apart during cooking, so I usually blend some of them to get a well-textured mixture. You can choose the size of the pasta you want. If you are making the pasta yourself, you can cut it bigger or smaller; they will both go well with this sauce. Barba di frate (also known as *barba del negus* or *agretti*) is an extremely tasty vegetable that grows wild along the coasts of Italy and today it is also widely cultivated. Its use in the past didn't have much to do with cooking: when burned it makes soda ash. That's right, the exact same one used to make soap.

FOR 4 PEOPLE

3 cups barba di frate (spinach can be used a substitute, though not as sharp)

1 garlic clove

Extra-virgin olive oil

Fresh chili pepper, finely chopped, to taste

Salt

2 cups chickpeas, cooked

A pinch of saffron

1 pound fresh tagliatelle pasta (page 22)

Freshly ground black pepper

Remove the toughest, woodiest parts, then wash the barba di frate and place it in a large pan, without drying it too much.

Add the garlic, oil, chili pepper, and a bit of salt and then cook it over medium heat for around 15 minutes. It should still be al dente.

Blend half of the chickpeas, then add all of the chickpeas to the pan with the vegetables. Dissolve the saffron in some water in a cup and add it to the vegetables.

Meanwhile, cook the tagliatelle until al dente, drain, and sauté it for a few minutes together with the vegetables, then drizzle with a little oil and sprinkle a generous amount of ground pepper on top along with a little of the pasta cooking water so that the pasta is smooth and not too dry.

Barba di frate is also delicious boiled or steamed, with just a little oil and lemon dressing.

TRENETTE PASTA WITH PESTO

In Liguria, this kind of pasta was known as *trenette avvantaggiate*— "the favored pasta"—as it cost less since it was considered a second-rate pasta, due to the bran in the flour. In actual fact, trenette pasta was considered to be a real delicacy, because its rough texture would soak up the pesto wonderfully. That is why this definition has permeated culinary memory, even though you can't find this kind of pasta any more and durum wheat trenette is usually used instead. This story brings to mind *stroncatura*—a traditional pasta from Calabria with the same characteristics, but that is always eaten *all'agghiu e l'ogghiu*: with garlic, oil, and chili pepper. Just like the trenette of times gone by, it is rough and dark and you can still find it "under the counter" today, wrapped in brown paper, the old-fashioned way.

FOR 4 PEOPLE

Salt
⅔ cup green beans
1 large potato, diced
1 pound trenette pasta
1 batch Pesto (page 17)
Extra-virgin olive oil
Freshly ground black pepper

Place a large pot filled with a generous amount of salted water on the stove, and when it comes to a boil, add the green beans.

After 5 to 6 minutes, add the potato and return to a boil. Add the trenette pasta and when it's al dente, drain together with the vegetables, making sure to keep some of the cooking water.

Mix in the pesto, adding a small ladleful of the pasta cooking water if the pasta is too dry.

Stir well and serve. Place the oil on the table, to drizzle on top to taste, along with the pepper grinder.

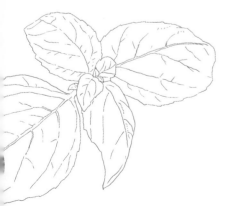

Pesto is also used with testaroli pasta, a specialty of the Lunigiana region. This is a large, disk-shaped pasta made with water and flour and cooked on the stove on a *testo* (a traditional kind of pot made from terra-cotta or, more commonly, cast iron, which cooks in the same way as an oven). Once ready, the testaroli is cut into strips and boiled like pasta.

SPAGHETTI WITH WILD ASPARAGUS

Wild asparagus is slightly more bitter than the cultivated kind, yet has a stronger aroma. During the spring, wild asparagus is easy to find in the woods, as well as in the hills, nestled in the fields, amid thorny shrubs. Best not to mistake it for butcher's broom, which only has a single bloom on the end and a purple stem: It is much more bitter and will completely ruin the sauce. It's best to blanch it first and then make a classic frittata—vegan, of course.

Snap the asparagus with your hands until you get to the toughest part, which you should discard.

Heat some oil in a large skillet. Brown the onion, then add the asparagus and a bit of salt and let it develop some flavor for a few minutes.

Add the tomato sauce, season with salt and pepper to taste, then cook the sauce until the asparagus is tender and the oil starts to rise to the surface. This should take around 25 minutes.

Cook the pasta, drain it when it is al dente, and add it to the sauce. Sauté it for a few minutes and then serve.

According to the rules of fine cuisine, you should separate the tips from the rest of the asparagus, cook them alone, and then add them in at the end. I almost never do this, and even if a few tips are a little damaged, for me it's fine just the same.

1 bunch wild or pencil asparagus

Extra-virgin olive oil

½ sweet red onion, sliced

Salt

2 cups tomato sauce

Freshly ground black pepper

1 pound spaghetti

FOR 4 PEOPLE

MACCHERONCINI PASTA WITH PUNTARELLE GREENS

Puntarelle greens are the gastronomic superstars of some very popular dishes in Rome, even if—in actual fact—you'll find that the best ones on the market come from Puglia, especially during this season. These crunchy, water-rich shoots grow in the center of a variety of Catalonian chicory when it has sprouted. Puntarelle greens are usually eaten raw, cut into thin strips after an ice bath, which makes them curl up and lose their bitter taste. But they are even better cooked and served on pasta, because they are slightly bitter and very appetizing. The maccheroncini pasta that I'm talking about is the kind that is traditionally eaten in Southern Italy. I would help my mom when she was making it and we'd roll the pieces of semolina pasta around knitting needles coated in flour. We never owned the special tool, and, quite frankly, I think hardly anyone has one at home.

FOR 4 PEOPLE

- 1 pound puntarelle greens (or chicory)
- Extra-virgin olive oil
- 2 garlic cloves
- A handful of pitted olives, chopped
- Dried chili pepper, finely chopped, to taste
- Salt
- 1 pound maccheroncini al ferretto pasta

Separate the puntarelle greens, cut them into thin strips, and allow them to soak in a bowl of ice water for half an hour, until they curl up.

Heat 2 to 3 tablespoons of oil in a large skillet along with the garlic, then throw in the puntarelle greens and fry them gently for a few minutes, stirring with a wooden spoon.

Add the chopped olives and chili pepper, season with salt, and continue to simmer, until the vegetables are tender but still crunchy, adding a little bit of water so that they remain moist enough.

Cook the pasta, drain when it is al dente, and sauté for a few minutes in the skillet with the puntarelle greens before serving.

To add a touch of crunchiness, you could sprinkle the plates with toasted almond flakes or almond slivers.

LASAGNE WITH ASPARAGUS

This is a lighter lasagne recipe: just three layers and lots of béchamel sauce and vegetables. Lasagna noodles made without eggs are less porous, so they absorb less sauce, but make up for it with their beautiful texture on the palate. On the other hand, eggs are traditionally used when making fresh pasta in the Emilia Romagna region, while the farther south you go, the more pasta dough is prepared with water and flour only, usually mixed with durum wheat semolina. I think that béchamel pairs beautifully with vegetables, a little less so with tomatoes. That's why it's better to have some fun making lasagne with seasonal vegetables, even by adding more than one, avoiding the classic lasagne that would ultimately just be a substitute.

FOR 4 PEOPLE

2 bunches asparagus

Extra-virgin olive oil

Salt and freshly ground black pepper

2 spring onions, sliced (green tops included)

1 batch Béchamel Sauce (page 18)

12 lasagna sheets (page 22)

Preheat the oven to 400°F.

Break the asparagus by hand to the point where they break less easily, then set the harder stems aside.

Heat a little oil in a large skillet. Lightly fry the asparagus with a pinch of salt and pepper, together with the green onions. Allow them to gradually cook by slowly adding warm water and more salt, if necessary.

Meanwhile boil the reserved asparagus stems in a small pot and, when they are soft, puree them through a food mill and then mix the resulting pulp with the béchamel sauce.

Blanch the lasagna sheets in a large pot of boiling, salted water for a few minutes, then remove them with a slotted spoon and lay them out to dry on top of a cotton cloth.

Cover the bottom of a 9-by-13-inch baking pan with a bit of béchamel sauce, then lay out four sheets of lasagna, and top with a layer of béchamel sauce and one-third of the asparagus.

Create two more layers in the same way and bake the lasagne until it forms a golden crust.

Béchamel sauce with asparagus will be a little greenish . . . yet oh so delicious.
Add a little olive oil to the pasta water to prevent any sticking during cooking.

SPRING RISOTTO

This is a veritable celebration of color, made with freshly picked vegetables, which are added at the end to avoid altering their fresh and delicate taste. This risotto is truly an ode to spring. Arrigo Cipriani knew that all too well, the man who practically invented it and made it one of the specialties at Harry's Bar in Venice. I've never been a great fan of rice. I married a Milanese man who, of course, is obsessed with it, and we always end up in the same debate: I tell him that in my house we ate rice when we were sick and he tells me that it is no wonder because I'm from the south, and he's probably right. However, amid the laughter and sneers of the whole family in Milan, I've learned to make an "okay" risotto over the years and I have also learned to appreciate it. I must—grudgingly—admit that I love this risotto.

FOR 4 PEOPLE

1 bunch asparagus

2 small baby carrots, diced

2 zucchini, diced

Extra-virgin olive oil

1 spring onion, chopped

1¾ cups Vialone Nano
or Carnaroli rice

1 cup dry white wine

About 4 cups Vegetable
Stock (page 17)

Salt and freshly ground
black pepper

Chopped parsley, for serving

Cut off the tips of the asparagus and break the most tender part of the stems into small pieces.

Heat a little oil in a large skillet. Sauté the asparagus, carrots, and zucchini until they soften but do not darken in color. It should take around 10 minutes.

Heat about 2 tablespoons of oil in a large pot and sauté the spring onion until it becomes transparent.

At this point, add the rice and stir until each grain is coated in oil, and then add the white wine and simmer until reduced. Start adding the stock gradually as it is absorbed. When the rice is half cooked, toss in the vegetables. Season with salt and pepper to taste, then cook, adding additional stock little by little.

Take the risotto off the heat when it is still al dente and serve with a sprinkle of chopped parsley on top.

If you want to do something *pissera*, as they say in Florence (that is, a little over the top), garnish the dish with edible flowers, such as rosemary, borage, or calendula.

GIUDIA ARTICHOKES

Beautiful and famous, Giudia Artichokes represent the pièce de résistance of Roman cuisine. To be exact, they came to be in the ghetto of Rome, invented by Jewish housewives and eaten after the Yom Kippur fast. Naturally, we begin with the Roman artichoke. There are endless fields around Ladispoli and Civitavecchia. In Rome they are called *cimaroli* or *mammole*. They are delicious, tender, without fuzz and thorns, and fry well. This is not complicated to cook, but you need to pay attention because you have to deal with the sizzling oil, which must be hot, but not too hot, and above all, there must be enough to almost cover the artichokes.

FOR 4 PEOPLE

4 Roman artichokes (mammole)

Fresh lemon juice

Peanut oil, for frying

Salt and freshly ground black pepper

Remove the outer leaves of the artichokes, leaving only a piece of the stem. Use a sharp knife to trim the hard tip of the leaves on each artichoke, twisting it gradually, cutting with a spiral movement, working from the outside in. By doing so, you will gradually reach the innermost leaves that have the toughest part at the top. Eventually, the artichokes will look more or less like a rosebud. Now, peel the stem and the base of the artichoke, cutting away the stumps of the outer leaves that you removed earlier.

Lightly press the artichokes down against a work surface so that they open a bit, then submerge them in a bowl of cold water with some lemon juice for an hour or so. Finally, drain them well upside down and dry them.

Choose a pan that is big enough for the artichokes and one with high sides. Heat the oil in a large, deep skillet to a temperature that is a little lower than usual for frying (280° to 300°F), then submerge the artichokes. Cook them for around 10 minutes, and then remove them with a skimmer.

Spread the leaves apart ever so slightly, sprinkle with salt and pepper to taste, lightly spray with a bit of water, and throw them into the hot oil again, keeping them upside down for about 1 minute. This causes the outer leaves to open and they become crispy and delicious.

Remove the artichokes with the skimmer, place them upside down once more to remove any excess oil, and then serve.

Olive oil is actually best for the frying, but the artichokes also turn out delicious with vegetable oil.

FENNEL IN TOMATO SAUCE

You may not know this, but fennel comes in both male and female versions. The males are a little round and meaty, whereas the females are more fibrous and a bit longer. That's why it's better to eat the male ones raw and cook the female ones. I think that fennel is a wonderful vegetable. However you want to make them, they are scrumptious and they grow all year round! If the fennel is fresh, I even like them boiled because they are still fragrant. It may seem incredible, but my vegan friends were amazed the first time I prepared fennel with tomato sauce: hardly anyone ever thinks to put fennel together with tomato and yet it is great and turns out very tasty!

Preheat the oven to 400°F.

Remove the outer leaves and the tops from the fennel, and then cut the bulbs into wedges that are not too big.

Arrange them in a large baking dish together with all the other ingredients, except the oil, adding salt and black pepper to taste.

Add a drop of water, drizzle with the oil, and mix it all with your hands to evenly incorporate.

Cook them in the oven at 400°F for about 30 minutes until they become tender and golden.

These fennel bulbs come out quite well even if you cook them on the stove.

6 fennel bulbs
2½ cups peeled, drained, and crushed tomatoes
A handful of brined capers, rinsed
A handful of pitted olives
1 garlic clove, crushed
A pinch of fresh oregano leaves
Crushed dried chili pepper, to taste
Salt and freshly ground black pepper
Extra-virgin olive oil

FOR 4 PEOPLE

PIE OF GREENS

Barba di frate (opposite-leaved saltwort, or agretti) is a rustic vegetable, yet it is delightful in slightly more elaborate dishes. It grows in small bunches of long, green needles with woody stems. We only eat the green part and it must be washed well because it holds on to many residues from the sandy soil it grows in. This pie is very simple as far as ingredients go and is easy to prepare, but the addition of béchamel makes it soufflé-like and you are sure to make a great impression. Barba di frate has a consistency that is a little "rough," is very pleasing to the taste, and boasts a strong, decisive flavor that is extremely satisfying.

FOR 4 PEOPLE

Extra-virgin olive oil

Vegan bread crumbs

1 pound barba di frate
    or spinach

1 spring onion, sliced
    (green tops included)

Salt and freshly ground
    black pepper

1 cup Béchamel Sauce (page 18)

Preheat the oven to 400°F. Oil a 10-inch round baking dish and sprinkle it with bread crumbs.

Put the greens together in a large skillet with the spring onion.

Add salt and pepper to taste and cook until al dente, so that the barba di frate doesn't release too much of its water. It should take around 15 minutes.

Then add the béchamel sauce. Pour the mixture into the prepared baking dish.

Bake until it forms a nice golden crust, around 10 minutes.

Serve hot.

Serve with a mildly spicy tomato sauce, well blended to make it smooth and even.

ONION AND OLIVE FRITTATA

In my house, we eat onion frittata with small, colorful olives: a piece of frittata and then an olive, after which you spit out the pit. When my mother used to make it, we would count the pits at the end to see who had eaten more olives. This frittata is usually made with just the green tops of the fresh baby onions, cut into small pieces and sweated in a little oil. Our Easter lunch—usually a picnic—was never without it, and we certainly did not eat sandwiches, but rather oven-baked pasta and eggplant Parmesan. I mean . . . we are southerners! Being that there are no eggs in this, it will make you think of a huge fritter more than a frittata, but I promise you it is delicious all the same.

Slice the baby onions into rounds and cut their green tops into 1-inch pieces. Sweat these in a medium, nonstick skillet over medium heat with a little oil and a pinch of salt, stirring often and moving the pan since the ends tend to burn easily.

Beat the flour into the cold water in a mixing bowl to make a runny batter. Then add the parsley, saffron, and some salt and pepper.

Pour this batter into the pan with the baby onions, as you would with eggs, turning it to distribute it evenly.

You can turn the frittata over to cook it on the other side, or you could fold it and cook it for a little longer.

Serve it with olives on the side.

Like many frittatas, this one tastes wonderful either hot or cold.

1 bunch fresh baby onions

Extra-virgin olive oil

Salt

¾ cup all-purpose flour

Cold water

1 bunch flat-leaf parsley, chopped

A pinch of saffron

Freshly ground black pepper

A handful of olives

FOR 4 PEOPLE

VEGETABLE AND POTATO SAUTÉ

The pan is a great friend of vegetables, as it cooks them quickly, making them crunchy on the outside and tender on the inside. The trick is to add the salt at the end, when the vegetables are already sautéed, otherwise they will soften up right away or break in pieces. By using this method, they remain intact, keeping their natural color and—most important—they keep their flavor. The pan must be iron, aluminum, or copper—all materials that are great conductors of heat and guarantee the right temperature for perfect cooking. I've always used a cast-iron skillet; the blacker it becomes, the better it cooks. It has to be dried thoroughly on a flame after washing, otherwise it will rust.

FOR 4 PEOPLE

Extra-virgin olive oil

2 bell peppers, chopped

2 eggplants, sliced

4 medium potatoes, peeled and cut into small wedges

2 plum tomatoes, diced

Dried chili pepper, finely chopped, to taste

Salt and freshly ground black pepper

Heat 3 to 4 tablespoons of oil in a large, deep skillet, then toss in the bell peppers and the eggplant slices, which should not be too big. Cook them over high heat, stirring frequently, so that a nice crust forms, and then lower the heat for a few minutes to allow them to soften. Remove them with a skimmer and set aside.

Using the same oil over high heat, sauté the potato wedges quickly, turning often, until they become soft. This will take around 15 minutes.

At this point, put the other cooked vegetables into the skillet, stir, and allow them to cook for a few minutes, then make some room and add the tomatoes. Leave them to soften for a moment, then crush them with a fork, add some chili pepper, and cook for 1 to 2 minutes more. Stir this sauce into the vegetables, using a wooden spoon.

Season with salt and black pepper, and cook for another 5 minutes over high heat, moving the skillet a lot so the flavors blend with one another and the vegetables don't burn.

These vegetables are delicious hot, but absolutely sublime cold, even the next day. They are also excellent for filling sandwiches with crusty bread: You've got to try it!

ROMAN VEGETABLE SAUTÉ

Fava beans and peas steal the show in this recipe. They used to plant them amid the grape vines to nourish the soil and harvest them as they sprung up, still oh so tender. That's why they ended up in the pot with artichokes, where they were cooked quickly. Some people prefer their Roman vegetable sauté to be a bit watery, almost like a soup. Others prefer to reduce it and serve it as a vegetarian main dish or as an appetizer. The truth is that, as with all rustic fare, there is no hard-and-fast rule. Everyone makes it the way they like and it is always a truly delicious dish, reminding us of the peasant pearl of wisdom: simple is best.

FOR 4 PEOPLE

2 Roman artichokes
  (mammole)

Fresh lemon juice

Extra-virgin olive oil

2 spring onions, finely sliced

2 cups peas, shelled

2 cups fava beans, shelled

1 head romaine lettuce,
  cut into strips

½ cup dry white wine

Lesser calamint or fresh mint

Salt and freshly ground
  black pepper

Clean the artichokes, slice them, then let them soak for a while in a bowl of water with some lemon juice.

Heat a little oil in a large pan, sauté the spring onions, and once they become transparent, toss in the artichokes. Add the peas and fava beans after 5 minutes. Cook them over low heat for about 10 minutes, then add the lettuce and wine. Simmer until the wine reduces, then add the mint, cover the pan, and cook for about 20 minutes, remembering to add salt, to taste, only at the end, stirring occasionally.

Sprinkle some pepper on top and serve the sauté warm.

This dish is known as *vignarola romana* in Italian. A *vignarolo* was someone who grew fruit and vegetables, which gives us another possible explanation for the name of this dish.

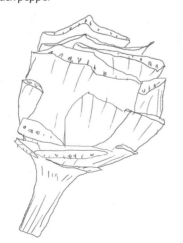

BREADED AND FRIED ASPARAGUS

Did you know that the part of the asparagus that we actually eat is known in scientific terms as the shoot? The shoots are the sprouts of the plant, which are collected when they stick out of the ground and are still tender. When breading them, you need to choose fairly large, fleshy asparagus: the violet asparagus of Albenga would be perfect, but even the white ones from Bassano or the ubiquitous green asparagus are fine. What matters is that they are big. Made in this manner, they are eaten one after the other, so when making an abundant main course be sure to put at least four or five on each dish, perhaps on a lovely bed of mixed salad with tomatoes, too.

Remove the toughest part of the asparagus, then blanch them in a pot of boiling, salted water for a few minutes.

Mix the flour with enough cold water in a bowl to get a smooth, even batter, and then add a little salt.

Dip the asparagus into the batter and then straight into the bread crumbs, making sure to press down firmly.

Heat the oil in a deep skillet, fry a few breaded asparagus stalks at a time, and then place them on paper towels when they are done, to absorb any excess oil.

Serve with a sprinkle of salt on top.

If you so desire, look for a vegan product on the market that replaces egg yolk. You could use it instead of the batter.

At least 20 large, fleshy asparagus stalks

Salt

1¼ cups all-purpose flour

Cold water

Vegan bread crumbs

Peanut oil for frying

FOR 4 PEOPLE

GREEN BEANS IN TOMATO SAUCE

Be careful—stewed green beans can be really awful if not cooked properly. The number one rule is to buy freshly picked green beans that are very tender. By doing so, you can apply the second fundamental rule: To get tasty stewed green beans that are still crunchy, it is crucial that you be able to cook them without adding water. I learned to make them quite well from a nanny who would help us at our seaside home and who came from Versilia. I was always with her when she cooked and I learned lots. After she had put the right amount of onion needed to add some flavor and the right amount of tomato to give it a bit of color and moisture, she would put the lid on the pot and say, "It will cook by itself," which meant that at that point all you had to do was remember to stir the green beans every now and then.

FOR 4 PEOPLE

1½ pounds green beans
   (burrini if possible)
½ small onion, sliced
¼ cup extra-virgin olive oil
Salt
2 ripe tomatoes

Trim the beans, rinse them, and put them in a large pot along with the onion, olive oil, and salt.

Cook them, covered, over high heat, sweating them a little, without letting them soften immediately. Make sure to stir often with a wooden spoon, otherwise they will stick to the bottom of the pot. When the beans are halfway cooked, after about 15 minutes, break the tomatoes into midsize pieces with your hands and add them to the green beans.

Cook the beans over low heat for a bit longer, until they become tender and slightly browned. This should take about 15 minutes.

They are also excellent cold.

It is important not to overdo it with the onion and tomato, otherwise the dish will become something different altogether.

BAKED SWISS CHARD

In the Calabrian dialect, Swiss chard is called *secari*. This is the slightly larger one that pops up spontaneously in vegetable gardens from one year to the next. My mother sometimes goes to the vegetable garden behind our house, picking one leaf here, another there, and comes back with a basket full of them. This recipe is part of the *ammollicata* series—this is the soft inside of bread. In Southern Italy, stale bread is used in almost everything to soak up the liquid released by cooked vegetables, but it is used—more than anything else—to give substance and texture to the palate. That is how Swiss chard can be turned into something like a vegetable pie, an excellent main dish.

Preheat the oven to 400°F.

Wash the Swiss chard and boil it in a large pot of salted water for 3 to 4 minutes, then drain it and cut it into pieces.

Oil a 3-quart baking dish, then add the Swiss chard, garlic, olives, oil, chili pepper, and salt.

Mix it all together with your hands, then sprinkle the bread crumbs on top, drizzle with a little bit of oil, and bake until it forms a nice crust. This will take about 20 minutes.

Like all *ammollicate* vegetables, this is delicious either hot or cold.

2 pounds Swiss chard

Salt

1 garlic clove, finely chopped

A handful of pitted baked olives, chopped

2 tablespoons extra-virgin olive oil

Dried chili pepper, finely chopped, to taste

Bread crumbs from inside of stale vegan bread

FOR 4 PEOPLE

CHOCOLATE CHANTILLY
WITH STRAWBERRIES

Thank Hervé This, the French physical chemist and chef who, in 1995, demonstrated that even chocolate can be whipped like Chantilly cream (whipped cream with sugar, for the French) since it has a similar structure to cream and a high fat content and contains an emulsifier, soy lecithin, which is added to better dissolve the sugar. This discovery practically marked a revolution in the world of chocolate, toppling one of the biggest taboos that said that water and chocolate were absolutely incompatible. Actually, it is true that if you put a few drops of water in a pot of melted chocolate, it will lump up right away and become grainy. But if you stick to the proportions set out by This, you'll get a smooth, silky mousse. As with cream (which is an emulsion of fat dissolved in water), the fats in chocolate must be approximately 34 percent of the water you add. So, you have to look at the food label of your chocolate bar to see what percentage of fat it contains and then carry out a math calculation: in other words, multiply the percentage of fat by 100, divided by 34, and you'll get the amount of water to be used (in grams), which can be rounded down.

FOR 4 PEOPLE

3.3 ounces vegan chocolate (70% cacao with 46% fat), chopped

½ cup water

2 cups strawberries

2 tablespoons sugar

Place the chocolate and water in a small, heavy-bottomed pan. Put it over low heat and stir the chocolate until it has melted and completely emulsified with the water.

Pour the mixture into a mixing bowl that you have placed inside an ice bath. Let it cool, then beat it at a high speed with an electric mixer until it begins to peak, changing to a color that starts to look like a mousse.

Be careful not to whip it too much or the mixture will become grainy. If that happens, start over from scratch, melting it, cooling it, and whipping it again.

Leave the mousse in the refrigerator for a few hours. Meanwhile, hull and slice the strawberries and infuse them in a bowl of sugar for half an hour. Serve the mousse with the sugared strawberries.

If you prefer a sweeter mousse, add 2 tablespoons of sugar to the chocolate.
For convenience, here again is the formula for calculating the amount of water, assuming 100 grams (3.3 ounces) chocolate: the percentage of fat in the chocolate bar x 100 ÷ 34 = grams of water to use.

CHERRY STRUDEL

I'll never forget the uncontrollable happiness that would wash over me and my siblings when we started to see the cherries at the greengrocers and my mother would finally buy them for us. We always counted them and would fight to the death to get a few more. Luckily, cherry season lasts long enough to get over this craving. The first would come from Puglia, which we called "the railways," because they used to ship them by train. Then from late May through July, we'd get the ripe Durone nero di Vignola variety, the most prized cherries ever, with an extremely sweet, firm pulp.

FOR 4 PEOPLE

2 cups cake flour (Italian "type 00"), plus more for dusting

A pinch of salt

1 teaspoon sugar

½ cup warm water

¼ cup vegan butter, plus more for toasting and brushing

2 tablespoons vegan bread crumbs

2 pounds cherries, pitted

½ cup vegan chocolate chips (70% cacao with 46% fat)

Sift the flour with the salt on a work surface to create a well. Then add the sugar. Knead in the water and butter until you get an even pastry dough. Knead vigorously, pounding the dough against the work surface occasionally, then wrap it in a cotton cloth and leave to rest for an hour or so, under a heated pot. (Rinse the pot with boiled water, then empty it and carefully dry it.)

Preheat the oven to 350°F.

Toast the bread crumbs in a skillet with very little butter.

Cover the work surface with a large cotton cloth that has been well floured. Roll out the pastry dough with a rolling pin, then slide your floured hands under the pastry and begin to enlarge it by gently pulling from the center outward, until you have a very thin sheet.

Brush the pastry with butter, sprinkle the bread crumbs on the side that is closest to you, then add the cherries, chocolate, and some more bread crumbs.

Using the cloth, roll the pastry over on itself and seal the edges thoroughly.

Use a brush to lightly brush the strudel with butter, slide it onto a baking pan lined with parchment paper, and bake about 40 minutes, until it gets a nice biscuit color.

You can replace the chocolate in the filling with ½ cup of toasted almond flakes.

BIANCOMANGIARE/ BLANCMANGE

White and oh so sweet, this is a typical Sicilian pudding. Here I'm giving you the Modica version, which is the simplest. Since the Middle Ages, throughout Europe, the term *blancmange*—*biancomangiare* in Italian—has referred to foods whose ingredients are mostly white. But, according to the customs of the time, these were recipes that mixed sweet and savory, combining chicken or fish with almonds, sugar, and milk. This dessert probably arrived in Sicily with the Arabs. It is made with almond milk, which is part of the everyday diet in the south, especially in summer. My grandmother would make almond milk now and then, after big meals, because it was refreshing. She would take a handful of almonds, peel them, then place them in cheesecloth and crush them with a hammer. She would submerge the cheesecloth with the almonds into a glass of water, moving it up and down to allow the white fluid that formed to drain out, which we just had to drink immediately.

Soak six individual plastic custard molds in cold water beforehand (it will be easier to get the puddings out of the molds).

Thoroughly mix the almond milk with the sugar and cornstarch in a large, heavy-bottomed pan.

Cut the vanilla pod lengthwise, remove the seeds, and add them to the mixture. Simmer over low heat, stirring with a wooden spoon until the mixture thickens.

Pour the cream you have made into the soaked and drained molds.

Leave to cool, then refrigerate for a few hours.

Turn out the blancmange and serve garnished with pistachios.

You can also flavor almond milk with lemon zest and ground cinnamon instead of vanilla.

1 quart almond milk
1 cup sugar
1 cup cornstarch
1 vanilla pod
Chopped pistachios, for garnish

FOR 6 PEOPLE

SWEET RICE FRITTERS

In Florence St. Joseph is called "San Giuseppe Frittellaio"—Fritter-Making St. Joseph. March 19 is his feast day (and, in Italy, Father's Day) and in Tuscany that is when they make these rice fritters. My mother, although not Tuscan, was still very on the ball when it came to celebrations and traditional foods, and so the night before you would find her boiling the rice, which was to rest overnight, and then she would spend the morning of St. Joseph's Day frying. These fried rice balls would then be shared around the apartment block, because almost all the mothers in the building would make them and swap them, spending the entire day talking and trying them, leaving all the front doors open. It was so lovely! It was truly another world. . . . This recipe has been a bit modified: the absence of eggs means that I have added a pinch of baking powder and I replaced the milk with rice milk.

FOR 4 PEOPLE

1 cup Arborio rice

2 cups rice milk

1 cup water

½ cup sugar, plus more for coating

A pinch of salt

Zest of 1 lemon

Peanut oil, for frying

2 tablespoons cornstarch

½ teaspoon baking powder

Bring the rice with the rice milk, water, sugar, salt, and lemon zest to a boil in a large pot.

Reduce the heat, cover, and cook over low heat until it has absorbed all the liquid, then let it stand overnight.

The next day, heat peanut oil in a large, deep frying pan. Stir the cornstarch and baking powder into the rice mixture, then pour the batter by the spoonful into the hot oil, frying a few fritters at a time.

Remove them with a skimmer, dry them on paper towels, and then roll them in sugar.

You can add raisins or a bit of rum to the rice for flavor.

PANNA COTTA

Even vegan panna cotta is an emulsion of fats in water, just like the cream made from animal milk. The process for making panna cotta is still the same, as are the other ingredients. You only have to choose the type of cream you would prefer: soy, oat, or coconut. Coconut cream has the most flavor and a strong taste, but if you use soy cream, which is more delicate, you can play around with spices and add a vanilla pod, a pinch of cinnamon, or saffron. You can even add loads of different garnishes: caramel, melted chocolate, a seasonal fruit coulis, or fresh fruit.

Mix the cream with the brown sugar in a small pot.

Take a small knife, slice the vanilla pod lengthwise, scrape out the seeds inside the pod, and add them to the cream mixture.

Bring to a boil. Meanwhile, dissolve the agar in the milk, and when the sugar is dissolved, add the agar mixture to the cream mixture and remove from the heat.

Divide the panna cotta among four single-serving ramekins, leave to cool. When the cream starts to solidify and pull away from the sides of the ramekins, refrigerate for at least 3 hours.

A coulis for garnish: Combine 1 cup of strawberries or raspberries plus 2 tablespoons of sugar and a few tablespoons of water. If necessary, bring to a boil in a pot and then blend.

2 cups soy cream
½ cup light brown sugar
1 vanilla pod
1 teaspoon agar
A drop of Plant-Based Milk (page 25)

FOR 4 PEOPLE

APPETIZERS

Summer Crostini, 70

with Marinated Zucchini

with Fresh Bean and Spring Onion

Pan Molle di Prato/Tuscan Tomato and Bread Salad

San Marzano Tomatoes au Gratin, 71

Fried Zucchini Blossoms, 72

Eggplant with Mint Sauce, 74

Panzanella Toscana/
Tuscan Bread Soup, 75

Bell Pepper Rolls, 76

Grilled Vegetable Salad with
Salmoriglio Sauce, 77

Pulicia's Pizza with Fresh Tomato
and Spicy Peppers, 78

Eggplant Fritters, 80

FIRST COURSES

Tomato Soup with Bread, 81

Linguine with Lettuce, 82

Tagliatelle with Fresh Beans, 83

Spaghetti with Romano Beans, 84

Baked Paccheri Pasta, 86

Spaghetti with Eggplant Parmesan, 87

Bucatini with Fresh Wild Fennel, 88

Rigatoni with Bell Pepper
and Celery Ragout, 89

Spaghetti with Pureed Tomatoes, 90

Rice Casserole with Potatoes
and Tomatoes, 92

SUMMER

MAIN COURSES

Eggplant Cutlets, 93

Eggplant and Zucchini Parmesan, 94

Spicy Eggplant, 95

Mixed Fried Vegetables, 96

Stuffed Round Zucchini, 98

Potatoes with Garlic and Oregano, 99

Vegetable-Stuffed Bell Peppers, 100

Caponata Siciliana with Eggplant,
Peppers, and Capers, 101

DESSERTS

Spiced Stewed Cherries, 102

Apricot Pudding, 104

Deep-Fried Fruit, 105

Plum and Hazelnut Pie, 106

Watermelon Ice, 107

SUMMER CROSTINI

Summer is the season in which Mother Earth is most generous, the weather is perfect, and we crave simple, wholesome foods. Our gardens overflow with vegetables and there is amazing variety. In the kitchen, the best choice is always the simplest, that which most enhances the available ingredients. Fantastic tomatoes, marvelously tender zucchini, oh so sweet onions, aromatic basil, salt and pepper to taste, and a dash of oil. What's missing? All you need to add is bread. Crostini and bruschetta are the answer to everything when it comes to filling your table with wonderful, tasty food. *Pan molle di Prato* is more of a salad on a slice of bread than a crostini. It's similar to *panzanella*, a Tuscan bread salad, except with more vegetables.

CROSTINI WITH MARINATED ZUCCHINI

- 4 small, tender zucchini
- ½ garlic clove
- 1 bunch flat-leaf parsley, chopped (reserve some for garnish)
- Juice of ½ lemon
- Extra-virgin olive oil
- Salt and freshly ground black pepper
- 4 slices vegan Tuscan bread, toasted

Use a mandoline to thinly slice the zucchini and then season with the garlic, parsley, lemon juice, oil, and salt and pepper to taste. Allow it to marinate for an hour in the refrigerator, then spread it over some slices of lightly toasted Tuscan bread. Drizzle a little more olive oil and a sprinkle of parsley on top before serving.

CROSTINI WITH FRESH BEANS AND SPRING ONION

- 1 cup cooked cannellini beans
- 1 baby spring onion, finely chopped (including some green tops)
- 4 slices vegan Tuscan bread, toasted
- Extra-virgin olive oil
- Salt and freshly ground black pepper

Spread the beans and spring onions on the bread. Season with olive oil, salt, and a nice sprinkle of pepper.

PAN MOLLE DI PRATO/ TUSCAN TOMATO AND BREAD SALAD

- 2 cups water
- ½ cup white wine
- A few basil leaves
- A few bay leaves (reserve some, shredded, for garnish)
- A little fresh rosemary
- 2 whole cloves
- 2 ripe tomatoes, finely sliced
- 4 radishes, finely sliced
- 1 sweet red onion, finely sliced
- 1 cucumber, finely sliced
- 1 celery stalk, finely sliced
- Extra-virgin olive oil
- Vinegar
- Salt and freshly ground black pepper
- 4 slices vegan Tuscan bread

Combine the water with the wine in a mixing bowl, then add the herbs and cloves, and soak for an hour or so. Put all the vegetables in a bowl, and season with oil, vinegar, and salt to taste. Working quickly, dip the slices of bread into the seasoned wine mixture and then lightly squeeze them, without breaking them. Arrange them on plates and cover with the seasoned vegetables. Garnish with the shredded basil leaves, then drizzle some more olive oil and grind some pepper. If you prefer bread that is slightly more rustic, you could choose a vegan whole wheat bread—it will be superb.

SAN MARZANO TOMATOES AU GRATIN

So red and fleshy, with that little point on the end that has made them legendary, yet the San Marzano tomato seems to have vanished, lost in the crowd of modern, bulky tomatoes designed to satisfy the distant markets. The San Marzano tomato is the king of sauces, the absolute best when it comes to making preserves, concentrates, and peeled tomatoes. This is pretty much the only tomato I use during the summer. For me, it's perfect cooked or raw, however you want to eat it. I'm a bit of a fanatic when it comes to tomatoes—I never buy tomatoes out of season, I hate date tomatoes, and I absolutely cannot stand vine tomatoes. In my family, tomatoes are a serious matter. We purposely go down to Calabria to make "the bottles" of sauce for winter and it is a ritual that takes place every year in the same way. We work with 200 to 250 pounds of tomatoes and make tomato sauce, peeled tomatoes, diced tomatoes with chili pepper, and sliced tomatoes with basil, which we eat in salads come winter.

Preheat the oven to 400°F. Lightly oil a baking sheet.

Slice the tomatoes in half and removes the seeds, sprinkle with salt, and place upside down on a cutting board to drain.

Mix the bread crumbs in a bowl with the garlic, capers, chopped olives, oregano, salt, and a little oil. Remember to rinse the capers thoroughly beforehand.

Fill the tomatoes with this mixture and place on the prepared baking sheet.

Drizzle with a little more oil and a sprinkling of pepper, then roast in the oven for about 20 minutes, until they are golden brown on the surface.

Extra-virgin olive oil
8 firm, ripe San Marzano or plum tomatoes
Salt
A handful of vegan bread crumbs (ideally made from stale bread)
½ garlic clove
1 teaspoon salted capers, rinsed
1 tablespoon chopped, pitted olives
A pinch of fresh oregano
Freshly ground black pepper

FOR 4 PEOPLE

They're delicious cold, too—actually, that's how I prefer them. In my opinion, a bit of dried chili pepper is better than ground pepper here, but I'll leave the choice up to you . . .

FRIED ZUCCHINI BLOSSOMS

There is neither heavy, "bready" batter nor egg in this recipe—simply zucchini flowers, water, and flour. There is always someone who is amazed when I make these fritters, because they're so good even though they are made from practically nothing, and the zucchini blossoms are almost treated with nonchalance. I wash them, rip them apart with my hands, place them in a mixing bowl, and then add a bit of flour and water, if needed, just enough to bind the mixture together. The fritters are never exactly the same and that is the beauty of it all. The ones my grandmother made were a bit different. Her batter was more even and moist. I, on the other hand, wet the blossoms and stir them just a little, because I discovered that they come out lighter and crispier this way. I learned this from my Japanese friend who made a fantastic tempura and I will always be grateful to her due to this.

FOR 4 PEOPLE

About 20 zucchini blossoms

1 bunch flat-leaf parsley, chopped

All-purpose flour

Salt

Cold water

Peanut oil, for frying

Remove and discard the stems and pistils from the blossoms, then wash them and place them in a mixing bowl without drying them.

Pull them apart with your hands, then add the parsley and a little flour, just enough to bind them a bit.

Season with salt and mix with a spoon, without overdoing it so as not to spoil the blossoms too much. Add just a little cold water, if needed.

Heat a good amount of oil in a large cast-iron skillet.

Drop spoonfuls of the fritter batter into the oil, a few at a time: You'll see that some of the batter tends to break off, but use the spoon to add it back to the fritter, just as you would with tempura.

Turn over the fritters with a pair of tongs, but be careful not to puncture them. Remove them from the oil when they are nice and crisp and place them on paper towels to drain any excess oil.

The fritters will not all be the same; some will have very crispy ends, others less so—but they will all be delicious!

Sometimes I add a bit of fresh chili pepper or a pinch of saffron to the batter.
If you don't have many blossoms, add some thinly sliced zucchini.

EGGPLANT
WITH MINT SAUCE

When I turned 50, I told my aunts that the only gift I wanted from them was that they make me a dinner consisting solely of eggplant. Thus they all went to get their hands on a crate of eggplants and each cooked her specialty, in large quantities. We call the eggplants in this recipe *a fungo*—literally "mushroomed eggplants"—because it is said that they look like fried mushrooms, and they were on the menu that night. This is one of my favorite recipes. In Calabrian cuisine, eggplants could almost be compared to meat. They are often served as the main course in place of meat during the summer because they have a nice texture and are even good in more elaborate recipes that are meant to be filling.

Remove the stems, then cut each eggplant lengthwise into four pieces, then in two the other way, so that you end up with eight pieces.

Place them in a large pot, cover with cold water and then bring to boil. Drain them when they begin to change color, which should take 2 to 3 minutes.

Leave them under something heavy for about an hour to get all of the water out: I usually leave them in the colander, covered with an upside-down plate, and then add a pot full of water on top to weigh the plate down.

Heat plenty of peanut oil in a deep skillet. Dip the eggplant pieces in the flour and fry them until they are golden on all sides. Remove with a skimmer and let dry them on paper towels.

Pour a little olive oil into a small pan, brown the garlic for a few seconds, then remove it and discard. Toss in the mint and vinegar and leave to reduce for about 1 minute, then remove from the heat.

Arrange the eggplant in layers on a tray, season lightly with salt, and then pour the mint sauce on top, making sure to cover all the pieces.

Let it sit for an hour in the refrigerator before serving.

3 oval eggplants
Peanut oil, for frying
All-purpose flour
Extra-virgin olive oil
1 garlic clove
1 bunch mint
½ cup vinegar
Salt

FOR 4 PEOPLE

These are delicious even without the sauce, warm or cold, with salt added just before serving.

PANZANELLA TOSCANA/
TUSCAN BREAD SOUP

As Aldo Santini says in *La cucina fiorentina*, his book on Florentine cuisine, panzanella—Tuscan bread soup—can be made in a hundred ways. The base is dry bread, which is why it is softened with water to revive it before adding the seasoning. I'm a fan of the classic version, the one made only with tomato, onion, plus, at the very most, cucumber, because if you add other vegetables it turns into a salad. The name derives from *pan* meaning "bread" in Italian and *zanella*, referring to the drainage channels between one field and another, which were always dry during the summer, where the farmers would eat this dish. It may seem a bit of a stretch but, out of all the stories that exist, this seems the most likely to me.

FOR 4 PEOPLE

2 cups stale vegan Tuscan bread (2 to 3 days old), cubed

2 tablespoons vinegar

1 tablespoon water, plus more for soaking the onions

2 sweet red onions, thinly sliced

Salt

5 ripe beefsteak tomatoes, chopped

1 cucumber, peeled and thinly sliced

1 bunch basil, shredded

Freshly ground black pepper

Extra-virgin olive oil

Place the bread in a bowl with the vinegar and water, letting it soak for about 10 minutes. Squeeze it thoroughly, then place it into a salad bowl, crumbling it up a bit.

Place the red onion in a small bowl of water and salt for about one hour to take away some of its bitterness and then mix together with the tomatoes, cucumber, and basil.

Season to taste with salt, pepper, and plenty of oil. Stir it thoroughly and leave the panzanella in the refrigerator for an hour before serving.

A friend of mine would slice the bread very thinly, then cut the tomatoes in half, sprinkle them with salt, turn them upside down on the bread, and leave them for a few hours. Doing so, the bread soaked up the moisture and absorbed all the flavor from the tomato.

BELL PEPPER ROLLS

Bell peppers are delicious, beautifully plump and colorful. In my opinion, they are the most flavorful summer vegetable. You can make them a thousand different ways, they always taste good, and they're easy to prepare. They are also excellent cold, so you can cook them ahead of time. Peppers add flavor to sauces and preserve perfectly, even when frozen. They are also extremely healthy, because if you eat them raw, not only are they crunchy and delicious but they are also filled with vitamin C. Too bad they sometimes "come back to visit you"! Unfortunately, for some people they are impossible to digest and literally just sit in the stomach; it seems that the fault lies in the outer skin. Don't worry, we're removing it in this recipe.

FOR 4 PEOPLE

Extra-virgin olive oil

2 red or yellow bell peppers

Salt

½ garlic clove

⅓ cup vegan bread crumbs

1 tablespoon ground almonds

1 tablespoon toasted pistachios

1 tablespoon raisins, soaked

A pinch of fresh oregano

1 bunch fresh dill, chopped

Freshly ground black pepper

Preheat the oven to 400°F. Lightly oil a baking pan.

Grill the whole peppers on a baking sheet, until the outer skin begins to peel away and is slightly charred.

Leaving the oven on, remove the peppers and let them rest, covered, for a few minutes so they are easier to peel. Peel the peppers and then cut into strips. Smear with oil and sprinkle with a tiny bit of salt.

Rub the garlic onto the bottom of a mixing bowl and discard, then toss in the bread crumbs, nuts, raisins, oregano, and dill. Add a drizzle of olive oil and salt and black pepper to taste, and then mix thoroughly.

Spread the bread crumb mixture all over the pepper slices, then roll them up.

Place the rolls on the prepared baking pan, placing them very close together, to prevent them from unraveling while cooking.

Drizzle some oil on top and then pop into the oven for about 15 minutes, until they are nicely roasted.

Bell pepper rolls are superb cold. You can add a few drops of vinegar, if you like.

GRILLED VEGETABLE SALAD
WITH SALMORIGLIO SAUCE

True salmoriglio sauce is an emulsion of oil and water mixed together, to which you add lemon juice and, last but not least, herbs. At home *u sarmurigghiu*—"salmoriglio" in Calabrian dialect—is made only with olive oil, oregano, and garlic, and it's used to season practically everything. This aromatic oil goes well with vegetables, especially if they are cooked on the grill. At my house, in the country-side, we fire up the outdoor grill with vine prunings, which make fine embers. We place the grill on top of the embers to cook the sliced eggplants, while the peppers are thrown right onto the hot embers and we turn them over with sticks until they are nicely roasted. This is an ancient method, known as *alla palmisana*, which refers to the village of Palmi, where it was created.

Preheat the oven to 400°F.

Prepare the salmoriglio sauce by mixing the olive oil, garlic, and oregano in a bowl.

Roast the peppers on a baking sheet in the oven until they are roasted and the outer skin begins to peel off. Take them out, allow them to sit, covered, for a few minutes, then peel and cut them into even slices.

Put the whole tomatoes in the oven on a baking sheet, taking them out as soon as the skin splits, then peel and crush them.

Cook the eggplant slices under the oven grill or on a gas stove, until they become tender; it will take about 10 minutes. Shred by hand.

Combine the peppers, eggplant, and tomatoes in a salad bowl.

Dress the vegetables with the salmoriglio sauce, season with salt to taste, and stir thoroughly.

Allow the salad to stand for a while before serving, so that it develops some flavor.

4–5 tablespoons extra-virgin olive oil
1 garlic clove, chopped
A pinch of fresh oregano
2 bell peppers
2 ripe plum tomatoes
2 purple eggplants, thinly sliced
Salt

FOR 4 PEOPLE

The oregano from Aspromonte is some of the very best, not to mention extremely fragrant. It has to be dried slowly in the shade, otherwise it will darken.

PULICIA'S PIZZA
WITH FRESH TOMATO
AND SPICY PEPPERS

Pulicia was a farmhand who worked on my grandfather's farm. She was so small that everyone called her *la pulce*—"flea" (*pulicia*, in the Calabrian dialect). Her family got by on very little and even when it came to pizza, she could only add what she had, often just fresh tomatoes, garlic, and fresh chili peppers. When my grandmother would fire up the bread oven, the neighbors would come to bake their pizzas, as was the custom then. Pulicia's pizza was always the one that everyone wanted to try, even if it gave off heat from how spicy it was. We have something of an emotional bond with Pulicia's pizza, which is why we still make it every time we turn on the oven, and we reminiscence about her while we eat it. Since I mean you no harm, I've come up with a version that is much . . . gentler.

FOR 4 PEOPLE

1 batch Pizza Dough (page 20)

6 ripe plum tomatoes

2 sweet or spicy fresh chili peppers, chopped

Salt

A generous pinch of fresh oregano

4 tablespoons extra-virgin olive oil

Preheat the oven to 400°F. Lightly oil a 10-by-15-inch pizza pan.

Roll out the dough on the prepared pizza pan, spreading it out with your hands, from the center outward, until you have almost covered the entire pan.

Remove the stems and the seeds from the tomatoes, cut them into little pieces, and spread them over the dough, crushing them a bit.

Add the chili peppers and a pinch of salt.

Sprinkle the oregano and a drizzle of olive oil on top, then place the pizza in the oven.

Allow the pizza to bake until the edges are a little darkened and the tomatoes have roasted slightly, which should take around 20 minutes. Before removing it from the oven, make sure that the bottom is cooked, lifting one side with a spatula.

Pulicia would also use a tiny bit of finely cut garlic and you can also add olives and capers. It is best to use gloves when handling hot chili pepper!

EGGPLANT FRITTERS

Some might argue that this book will ultimately be a feast of fritters! In fact, I'm including a bit too many, but you'll just have to forgive me: I grew up with fritters. The first thing that comes to my mind when I have to cook a vegetable is to cover it in flour and throw it in the pan. Eggplant is especially good for frying and you don't even have to be afraid of overdoing it because frying can also be light and healthy—in addition to being delicious—if you follow the rules.

FOR 4 PEOPLE

2 large purple eggplants

½ garlic clove, chopped

1 bunch flat-leaf parsley, chopped

Fresh chili pepper, finely sliced, to taste (optional)

Salt

All-purpose flour

Peanut oil, for frying

Remove the stems, then cut the eggplants into eight pieces. Place them in a large pot and cover with cold water.

Bring to a boil and let them cook for a few minutes, then drain and put them under a weight for an hour to help drain the water.

Tear them into strips with your hands, then put them into a mixing bowl together with the garlic, parsley, chili pepper (if desired), and salt. Stir thoroughly, then add enough flour to bind it all together: You should get a rather thick batter.

Heat a generous amount of oil in a deep skillet until very hot. Shape the fritters with a spoon and fry them in the oil. Remove with a skimmer when they are golden brown and place them on paper towels to drain any excess oil.

Serve hot or cold, with a sprinkling of salt.

When eggplant is cooked and seasoned in this way, it is also great as a salad. Simply add a drizzle of extra-virgin olive oil.

TOMATO SOUP WITH BREAD

All Italian children who were growing up in 1964 will remember Rita Pavone screaming at the top of her lungs, "Long live tomato soup and bread" in the guise of "Gian Burrasca" in a television drama based on the popular book by Vamba. Before that, I had never tasted it (I think I've already told you that I'm not Florentine) and didn't know whether I would like it. But I certainly wanted to try it because it was the most famous food at that time and had become the symbol of the revolt of oppressed schoolchildren against their cruel professors. It is a very frugal dish, made with stale bread, but it's a real delicacy because it makes the most of the few ingredients available, which vary a little from home to home. For a truly authentic tomato soup and bread, however, you always need to have Tuscan bread (i.e., without salt), the Florentine beefsteak tomato, and oil made from olives grown on the hills around Florence.

Heat a little oil in a large pot. Fry the garlic cloves and the "ginger" (that's what they call chili pepper in Florence) in the oil, add the tomatoes and basil and simmer over low heat for 10 minutes, then dilute with the stock.

Season with salt, bring to a boil, and toss in the bread. Cook for about 10 minutes, then remove from the heat and let it sit, covered, for an hour or so.

Every now and then stir with a whisk until it becomes soupy.

Heat the tomato soup and serve hot or lukewarm, with a drizzle of oil, and season to taste with salt and a good sprinkle of black pepper.

During the winter you can use canned peeled tomatoes.
Some people like to fry a sliced leek together with the garlic and chili pepper.

Extra-virgin olive oil

2 garlic cloves, crushed

Dried chili pepper, finely chopped, to taste

2 pounds ripe tomatoes, peeled, seeded, and diced

1 bunch basil, leaves torn

About 4 cups Vegetable Stock (page 17)

Salt

2 cups thinly sliced vegan stale bread (2 to 3 days old)

Freshly ground black pepper

FOR 4 PEOPLE

LINGUINE WITH LETTUCE

In this recipe you cook the pasta together with the vegetables and its stock, which gives it a smooth consistency similar to certain Thai dishes. Linguine with Lettuce is made with romaine lettuce, the type that is big and white on the inside and harvested from early spring until late fall. It is a sweet, crisp vegetable, rich in water, and therefore very refreshing. I eat it raw, leaf after leaf, dipped in salt as my father taught me. He would always tell me the same story about how, as a child, he would have to walk five miles to get to school, eating lettuce bought for a pittance from a street vendor.

FOR 4 PEOPLE

1 large head romaine lettuce, separated into leaves and torn into thirds

1 small zucchini, halved lengthwise, then cut into 1-inch pieces

1 garlic clove

2 ripe tomatoes, diced

A few basil leaves

Extra-virgin olive oil

Salt

½ pound linguine pasta, broken in two

Fill a pot for the pasta one-third of the way with water and bring to a boil. When it boils, add the torn romaine together with the zucchini, garlic, tomatoes, and basil. Add a splash of oil and a pinch of salt and cook until the vegetables become tender but are still al dente: It will take 10 to 15 minutes.

Toss in the linguine and continue to cook, stirring occasionally and adding a little water, if necessary.

The pasta and lettuce should remain soft, but not too soupy.

Serve with a drizzle of extra-virgin olive oil.

If you don't like garlic, remove before serving: eating it inadvertently is truly horrible.

TAGLIATELLE
WITH FRESH BEANS

This recipe calls for eggless tagliatelle pasta made with durum wheat flour—it is the only kind that goes well with freshly shelled beans. Use cannellini beans, or the big, flattened ones that are simply called *fagiole*—"beans," or even toscanelli beans, which are a bit smaller and rounder. To ensure you cook them right, follow the same rules that apply to dried beans, except for the soaking, which is not needed here. The essentials are to add salt and always cook over low heat. The water should just simmer ever so slightly or else the shell of the beans will get really tough and they will all split.

Put the beans in a large pot and fill it with cold water. Add the celery, garlic, and tomatoes, then cover and place on low heat and allow to slowly simmer until tender, about 40 minutes.

Cook the tagliatelle pasta and when it is half-cooked, drain it and toss it into the pot with the beans to finish cooking. The result should be a soft soupy mixture that can be eaten with a fork, but with a spoon at the ready to get the beans on the bottom.

Serve hot with a drizzle of oil. Place the salt, black pepper, and chili pepper on the table so that everyone can season it as desired.

Tagliatelle goes especially well with borlotti beans.
You can add a bit of chopped sage and rosemary before serving.

2 cups fresh white
beans, shelled

1 celery stalk, diced

1 garlic clove, chopped

4 ripe tomatoes,
roughly diced

⅔ pound Fresh Tagliatelle
Pasta (page 22)

Extra-virgin olive oil

Salt and freshly ground
black pepper

Dried chili pepper, finely
chopped, to taste

FOR 4 PEOPLE

SPAGHETTI
WITH ROMANO BEANS

Romano beans are a long, flat—sometimes too flat—type of snap bean that are usually stewed and eaten as a side dish. In reality, all beans can be eaten whole as long as they are young and still green on the plant. Actually, I'd say that the best are slightly on the purplish side and a little bent—I think the right name is *stortino di Trento*. They are full of flavor and have a thin skin, but they're hard to find. If you happen to get some that already have a few peas inside, all the better. Shell only the toughest ones. In Southern Italy, Romano beans are mainly eaten with pasta. This is the most traditional version and it is extremely filling, as it also includes potatoes and zucchini.

FOR 4 PEOPLE

2 pounds Romano beans
   or snap beans

2 garlic cloves

6 ripe tomatoes, diced

A few basil leaves

Salt

Extra-virgin olive oil

2 potatoes, diced

2 zucchini, cut into rounds (not
   too thin, or they'll fall apart)

½ pound spaghetti,
   broken in two

Trim the beans—if they are the flat and long, cut them into two or three pieces.

Fill a large pot one third the way with water and bring to a boil. When it boils, add the beans, one of the garlic cloves, one-sixth of the diced tomato, a few basil leaves, some salt and a splash of oil. Bring to boil, then lower the heat and leave to cook for about 10 minutes.

Add the potatoes and zucchini. When the vegetables are half-cooked, toss in the spaghetti and stir immediately.

In the meantime, crush the remaining diced tomatoes with a fork in a small pan with a bit of oil and the remaining garlic clove. Allow it to reduce a little, then add this sauce to the pasta, season with salt, and cook until done. Keep in mind that this dish should be soupy, not too thick.

Put the olive oil on the table so that everyone can add a drizzle of oil if they like.

The tomato sauce is not essential. You can add all the tomatoes at the beginning. The pasta will just have less sauce, but it will be delicious and flavorful all the same.

BAKED PACCHERI PASTA

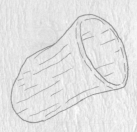

No one really knows whether they are Neapolitan, or if Calabria can really lay claim to the origins of these giant maccheroni. One thing is certain: *pacchera* means "a good slap" in both the Neapolitan and Calabrian dialects. *Schiaffettone* means the same thing and, in fact, it is another name for the very same pasta. I adore paccheri pasta, especially when they are covered in lots of sauce and with tomatoes. They should always be eaten al dente and, even when they are smooth, they hold a lot of sauce so they are perfect for baked dishes. Zucchini prepared this way are also sublime, with a sprinkling of salt.

FOR 4 PEOPLE

4 zucchini

Salt

Extra-virgin olive oil

1 sweet red onion, sliced

½ pound fresh tomatoes, peeled and crushed with your hands

Freshly ground black pepper

All-purpose flour

1 pound paccheri pasta

2 tablespoons vegan bread crumbs

Preheat the oven to 400°F.

Cut the zucchini lengthwise into thin slices, season with a little salt and leave in a colander for about half an hour.

In the meantime, heat a little bit of oil in a large skillet. Sauté the onion in the oil, add the tomatoes, and then season with salt and pepper. Reduce over low heat until the oil floats to the surface. This should take around 20 minutes.

Heat oil in a medium skillet. Lightly flour the zucchini, fry them in the oil, then place them on a paper towel to drain the excess oil.

Cook the pasta, drain it when it is still extremely al dente, and add some of the tomato sauce.

Spread some of the sauce over the bottom of a 9-by-13-inch baking pan, then put a layer of paccheri, a layer of sauce, and then a layer of zucchini. Continue until you run out of ingredients, finishing off with a few slices of zucchini for garnish.

Sprinkle some bread crumbs on top and bake until a golden crust forms.

You can also replace the zucchini with eggplant, fried in the same way.

SPAGHETTI
WITH EGGPLANT PARMESAN

We still call it Parmesan, even if this eggplant pasta recipe is a lot simpler to make and the only thing it has in common with traditional Parmesan is the eggplant. In the ancient recipe, the eggplant with all its frying oil—olive oil, naturally—was tossed into the tomato sauce and some bread crumbs were always added at the end, as is done between one layer of eggplant and another in the Parmesan. I think I've only ever eaten it once, prepared by my Aunt Dora who always cooked according to the old way. Delicious, yes, but perhaps a little heavier than what we are used to nowadays. But you can always give it a try.

FOR 4 PEOPLE

2 oval eggplants
Coarse salt
4 cups tomato sauce
Salt
Extra-virgin olive oil
Peanut oil, for frying
1 pound spaghetti

Cut the eggplants lengthwise into very thin slices, place them in a colander, and sprinkle coarse salt over every layer. Leave underneath a weight to drain the water for 1 hour.

In the meantime, place the tomato sauce in a large skillet with the olive oil and salt to taste and cook, covered, over low heat for about 30 minutes.

Squeeze the eggplant a bit, heat a generous amount of peanut oil in a medium skillet and fry the eggplant until it is nicely golden. Remove it with a skimmer, then place it on paper towels to dry.

When the sauce is almost cooked, add the eggplant. Cook for another 5 minutes and then remove from the heat.

Cook the spaghetti, drain it when it is still al dente, and pour a generous amount of eggplant sauce on top.

I never peel eggplants, even if you technically should in this recipe. You could also partially peel them, removing a few strips of the skin. If you prefer it, you could cut the eggplants into sticks.

BUCATINI
WITH FRESH WILD FENNEL

Come spring, the fields fill with wild fennel—it's everywhere, even along the streets. I always go and pick it at the beginning of the season when it is tall and green, with all its aromatic and crisp sprigs, so I can also add it to salads. Then, again, at the end of summer, when the umbrella-like tops fill with flowers and, last, in fall, I collect the branches that are filled with seeds and preserve them in bunches for the winter. Wild fennel is an extremely Mediterranean herb that adds character to many traditional dishes in southern Italy, Sicily first and foremost, where fennel picked in the sun-parched fields has an aroma that is truly amazing.

FOR 4 PEOPLE

¾ pound fresh wild or
    regular fennel

Extra-virgin olive oil

1 onion, sliced

2 tablespoons raisins, soaked

2 tablespoons pine nuts

A pinch of saffron

1 pound bucatini pasta

Salt

2 tablespoons toasted and
    chopped almonds

2 tablespoons toasted
    vegan bread crumbs

Blanch the fennel in a large pot in a generous amount of salted, boiling water, then remove it, blot it dry, and chop it coarsely. Set the cooking liquid aside.

Heat a little bit of oil in a large skillet. Sauté the onion in the oil, then add the fennel. Squeeze the raisins to remove any excess water and add to the onion along with the pine nuts.

Dissolve the saffron in a cup with a little bit of the fennel cooking liquid and add it to the rest. Cook over low heat for about 10 minutes, then season with salt.

Toss the pasta into the fennel cooking liquid and cook, drain it when it is still al dente, then transfer it to the pan with the sauce. Sauté it for a few minutes over high heat, adding some water, if necessary. Sprinkle with almonds and bread crumbs and serve.

Here's another option: Instead of sautéing it in the pan, season the bucatini in layers in an oven pan, sprinkled with some bread crumbs and almonds, then put in a preheated 400°F oven for about 20 minutes to develop some color.

RIGATONI
WITH BELL PEPPER
AND CELERY RAGOUT

More than any other vegetable, bell peppers are the epitome of summer. Celery, on the other hand, is the king of the vegetable garden: It's both a vegetable and an herb. Chopped celery is the king of sautés, stocks, and soups, while the stalks are the king of dips, salads, and many delicious dishes, even very elaborate ones. In this sauce the celery contrasts with the sweetness of the bell pepper with its distinctive and pungent flavor. I often make use of the leaves, too, which have an extremely intense flavor.

Clean the peppers and cut them into thin strips, then cut the celery into thin slices and coarsely chop some of the leaves.

Heat oil in a large skillet and toss in the bell peppers, celery, and garlic. Sauté over a low heat.

When they are fully sautéed, add the tomatoes, season with salt, and cook for a further 10 minutes.

Cook the pasta in a large pot, drain it when it is al dente, reserving the pasta cooking water, and fry in the skillet with the vegetable ragout for a few minutes, adding a good sprinkle of black pepper and a little of the pasta cooking water, if necessary.

Adding a small piece of dried chili pepper here would add a bit of pep—it goes amazingly well!

4 red and yellow bell peppers

1 small celery stalk, including its leaves

Extra-virgin olive oil

1 garlic clove, crushed

8 ripe plum tomatoes, diced

Salt

1 pound rigatoni pasta

Freshly ground black pepper

FOR 4 PEOPLE

SPAGHETTI
WITH PUREED TOMATOES

It's incredible, but it wasn't until the 19th century that tomatoes became part of everyday cooking. I really can't imagine a world without the tomato. I've raised three children on the tomato sauce that my parents make every year. In fact, when they were children, I would even add it to pasta cold, with just a drizzle of oil. That's how good it was. Sometimes they even drank it. In the same way, bread and tomato was my favorite summer snack and so it became theirs too—they had no choice. For me, it's all about culture. I can't stand the northern custom of adding three large spoonfuls of sauce to their pasta. "Pink" pasta dishes depress me. Pasta with tomato should be deep red and there should be a little sauce on the bottom of the plate that you can soak up with bread. This sauce is really a puree: While the pasta is cooking, you toss everything in a blender until it is well and truly emulsified.

FOR 4 PEOPLE

2 pounds ripe San Marzano plum or Florentine beefsteak tomatoes, diced

1 bunch basil

Fresh chili pepper or green bell pepper, to taste

Salt

6 to 8 tablespoons extra-virgin olive oil

1 garlic clove, smashed

1 pound spaghetti

Put the tomatoes, a few basil leaves, the chili pepper, salt, and plenty of oil into a blender. Blend on the highest setting until you get a lovely red sauce. Pour it into a mixing bowl and add the whole clove of garlic.

Cook the pasta in a large pot, drain when it is al dente, and toss it into the pureed tomato sauce, stirring well, then add a few more torn basil leaves and some more oil.

Remove the garlic clove and serve.

This pureed tomato sauce comes out extremely well when you use a classic, small-bladed immersion blender that comes with a beaker. Actually, any kind of food processor is fine, although the sauce will be less emulsified.

RICE CASSEROLE
WITH POTATOES AND TOMATOES

Tiella barese is a dish made with rice in a baking pan and even this vegan version is extremely filling and full of flavor. My mom made it like this, without the traditional mussels, probably because she thought it was lighter and less labor-intensive. Zucchini are also included in the traditional recipe and they work really well. It is essential that you cut the potatoes and onion very thinly or they will not cook properly and it will be a disaster. Some people like to parboil the potatoes before putting them in the baking pan, but I don't think this is a good idea as it will definitely change the taste.

FOR 4 PEOPLE

Extra-virgin olive oil

1 pound potatoes

1 large sweet red onion

3 zucchini

1 garlic clove

1 bunch flat-leaf parsley, chopped

1 pound plum tomatoes

1½ cups superfino rice, such as Carnaroli or Arborio

Salt and freshly ground black pepper

2 tablespoons stale vegan bread crumbs

Preheat the oven to 400°F. Lightly oil the bottom of a 9-by-13-inch baking pan.

Peel the potatoes, cut them into thin slices with a mandoline and place them in a bowl of water.

Cut the onion into very thin slices, and the zucchinis into rounds. Chop the garlic and parsley together. Slice the tomatoes.

Rinse the rice to get rid of the starch.

First, layer half of the onions in the prepared baking pan, then add one-third of the tomatoes. Sprinkle some parsley and garlic on top, then continue with half of the potatoes and half of the zucchini, a sprinkling of salt and pepper, and a drizzle of oil. Cover the mixture with the rice and some chopped parsley, then sprinkle once again with salt and pepper.

Make another layer with the onions, tomatoes, garlic, and parsley, then the potatoes and zucchini, ending with a layer of the tomatoes.

Dust the bread crumbs on top, then cover with cold water and a generous amount of olive oil.

Season with salt to taste and bake for around 45 minutes.

This rice casserole should be eaten warm, as soon as the rice has cooled and reduced a little. This makes it more compact when it is served.

EGGPLANT CUTLETS

In my house everything breaded is called a cutlet and there's always a good reason to add a few cutlets to the menu of the day. You make them for the children and for guests who you don't know very well, because everyone likes something that is breaded and fried. It's also good when you're worried that you won't have enough food. Cutlets are always perfect. They take a second to fry, and can be served hot or cold, for sit-down lunches or buffets, seated or standing, for picnics—you just can't go wrong. What's more, these eggplant "cutlets" are also perfect as an al fresco aperitif. You eat them with your hands and—if they are fried as they should be—they won't make your fingers greasy.

Mix the flour with enough cold water in a medium bowl to get a smooth batter and add a pinch of salt.

Cut the eggplant into horizontal slices, about ½ inch thick, and season with a little salt.

Dip them first in the batter, then in the bread crumbs, making sure to press them down firmly with your fingers to make them stick.

Heat a generous amount of oil in a large, deep skillet. Fry the breaded eggplant slices in the oil and remove them with a skimmer when they are golden brown.

Let them dry on paper towels, then serve with a sprinkle of salt on top.

¾ cup all-purpose flour

Cold water

Salt

2 oval eggplants

Vegan bread crumbs

Peanut oil, for frying

FOR 4 PEOPLE

EGGPLANT
AND ZUCCHINI PARMESAN

Eggplant Parmesan is my absolute favorite. My family has a long list of Parmesan specialists and we often discuss one aunt's compared to another's, my mom's compared to the legendary Parmesan of my grandmother. One thing is certain, it's a southern Italian dish, but we can leave to someone else whether its origins lie in Campagna or Sicily. I have a lot of doubts concerning whether the name refers to Parmesan cheese, as in my limited experience I've seen that this ingredient didn't make it to the south of Italy until the 1970s, or, if it was there, it was considered an abomination. It's more logical to think that they used local pecorino, caciocavallo, or provola cheeses. I prefer the theory that links parmesan to the dialectal term *parmiciana*, which is what the wooden slats of Venetian blinds are called in Sicily. And thus the dish consists of not just eggplant, but other vegetables such as zucchini as well, layered with sauce and then baked in the oven.

FOR 4 PEOPLE

2 large oval eggplants

Coarse salt

3 zucchini

2 cups tomato sauce

2 tablespoons extra-virgin olive oil

Salt

A few basil leaves

Peanut oil, for frying

2 tablespoons vegan bread crumbs

Cut the eggplants into very thin slices and place them in a colander, sprinkle some coarse salt on top, and leave them to drain off their water, with a weight on top, for around an hour.

Cut the zucchini into very fine slices, season with a little salt, and leave them to rest in a bowl for half an hour, or set them out to dry in the sun.

Meanwhile, preheat the oven to 400°F.

Reduce the tomato sauce in a large skillet with olive oil, salt to taste, and a few basil leaves.

Heat a generous amount of peanut oil in a large, deep skillet. Squeeze the eggplant and zucchini with your hands, then fry them, a few pieces at a time, in the oil. Remove them with a skimmer and leave them to dry on paper towels.

Spread a little sauce on the bottom of a 9-by-13-inch baking pan, then start building the layers, alternating the eggplant and zucchini with the sauce. Top it with a dusting of bread crumbs and a few basil leaves, then bake until a lovely golden crust forms. This should take 25 to 30 minutes.

I salt the eggplant, not to remove its bitterness (nowadays they are not so bitter), but so that it absorbs less oil during frying. Don't let yourself be fooled into grilling the vegetables instead of frying them; the end result may be good, but don't call it Parmesan.

SPICY EGGPLANT

I've given this recipe a new name because the dialectal term is practically untranslatable and does not convey the idea of the recipe. The eggplants are spicy because there are covered in fresh chili pepper, garlic, and capers: seasonings that enhance the flavor of the eggplant. They are really popular during the summer because you can make them right away. They only get better if you leave them in the refrigerator, so you can even make them long in advance. I like to eat them in the morning, around 11 a.m., in a sandwich, just so . . . cold from the refrigerator. They are really tasty and appetizing.

Preheat the oven to 400°F

Remove the stems, then cut the eggplants in two lengthwise and lay skin side down on a work surface. Use a sharp knife to cut across into the flesh of each half, without damaging the skin, so that you create a kind of grill.

Put the tomatoes in a mixing bowl. Add the garlic, capers, basil, oregano, chili pepper, salt to taste, and the oil.

Fill the eggplant halves with the tomato mixture, trying to nudge it into the cuts you made with the knife.

Place them close together on a rimmed baking pan, then pour a little water over them, drizzle with some oil and add a pinch of salt, then put them in the oven, covered.

Every so often, use the back of a fork to press them down, so as to push the tomato in further, gradually, as the eggplant softens. If the tomato falls out, just put it back onto the eggplant with a spoon.

You'll know they're ready when they are soft and the water has been completely absorbed. This will take around 25 minutes.

4 small, long eggplants
10 ripe plum tomatoes, diced
½ garlic clove, chopped
1 tablespoon salted capers, rinsed
A few basil leaves, chopped
A pinch of oregano
Fresh chili pepper, finely chopped, to taste
Salt
3 tablespoons extra-virgin olive oil

FOR 4 PEOPLE

MIXED FRIED VEGETABLES

Here are some good rules to follow when it comes to deep-frying at home. Choose a pan that is not too big and has high edges, made from a metal that conducts heat well. I still use a cast-iron pan, even if it's hard to clean and tends to rust. Fill it with oil, at least halfway, and start frying only when the oil has reached a temperature of around 350°F, and when you submerge a piece of food in it, it floats, sizzling to the surface right away, but before the oil starts smoking. Fry a few pieces at a time so that you don't lower the oil temperature, and remove them with a skimmer, taking care to not puncture them. Dry the fried food on paper towels and never cover them while they are still hot—condensation forms and softens the fried goodies. Try and toss the same-size portions into the pan, and never season with salt before frying! Choose either extra-virgin olive oil or peanut oil. Olive oil has a strong taste and is expensive. Peanut oil, on the other hand, leaves no flavor and has a higher smoking point.

FOR 4 PEOPLE

1¼ cups all-purpose flour

Sparkling water

Salt and freshly ground
   black pepper

Seasonal vegetables, such as:

  1 oval eggplant

  1 sweet red onion

  2 zucchini

  8 zucchini blossoms

  4 bunches of 3–4 cherry
     tomatoes on the vine

Peanut oil, for frying

10 giant sage leaves

Mix the flour in a bowl with the amount of sparkling water needed to get a smooth batter, without stirring too much. Season with salt, add a sprinkle of pepper to taste, then leave it to rest in the refrigerator for an hour.

Cut the eggplant horizontally into very thin slices, the onion into rings, and the zucchini into sticks. Clean the zucchini blossoms, removing the pistil from the inside. Leave the cherry tomatoes on the vine.

Heat the oil in a large, deep skillet, as described in the headnote.

Toss the vegetables and the sage into the batter, then submerge them, a few at a time into the hot oil, stirring once only.

Remove them with a skimmer and place them onto paper towels to absorb any excess oil.

Serve the fried vegetables piping hot, with a sprinkle of salt.

Another good system is to dip the slightly damp vegetables into the flour, then submerge them in the oil: They will be delicious and light, but this won't work with cherry tomatoes.

STUFFED
ROUND ZUCCHINI

Make sure you choose zucchini that are not too big—otherwise they will have absolutely no flavor—and that they are fresh, with firm, compact flesh—otherwise they will be bitter. Round zucchini, when they are freshly sprouted and still have their blossoms attached, are delicious even just pan-fried with a little salt. For this recipe use a teaspoon to hollow them out, as it is easier to follow the round shape. I prefer to fill them without parboiling them first, as many people do (of course, they cook faster this way, but they lose their flavor). Stuffed zucchini are delicious cold, too, but I would say that they are better eaten at least at room temperature as they have a lot more flavor.

FOR 4 PEOPLE

4 round zucchini

½ cup tomato sauce

Extra-virgin olive oil

Salt

⅓ cup stale vegan
   bread crumbs

A handful of pitted
   olives, chopped

1 bunch flat-leaf parsley,
   chopped

½ garlic clove, finely chopped

Freshly ground black pepper

Cut off the ends, then slice the zucchini lengthwise in two. Hollow out the centers with a teaspoon, taking care to not puncture the skin, and reserve the flesh.

Reduce the tomato sauce in a medium pan on low heat with a little oil and a pinch of salt.

Chop the zucchini flesh and mix half the flesh in a bowl with the bread crumbs, chopped olives, parsley, garlic, salt and pepper to taste, and a drizzle of oil.

Pour a little warm water and some oil into the bottom of a heavy-bottomed pan with low sides. Season the hollowed-out zucchini with salt, drizzle a splash of oil on top, and fill them with the bread crumb mixture. Place them close together on the prepared pan, then pour the tomato sauce over each zucchini.

Cook them, covered, over low heat until they are soft and the bread in the filling has puffed up.

I prefer cooking these zucchini on the stove, but they also come out great baked in a 400°F oven. While they are cooking, baste them with sauce from the bottom of the pan every now and then, scooping it up with a spoon.

POTATOES
WITH GARLIC AND OREGANO

With this recipe we travel to the Basilicata region of Italy. The Italian name for the recipe is *patate raganate*. *Raganate* is a strange word, and all it means is that the *patate*—"potatoes"—have been seasoned with the spectacular oregano that grows wild around those parts. Oregano, the splendor of the mountains (from the Greek *óros*/mountain and *gános*/splendor), is a magical herb—it makes even the simplest dishes appetizing and the vegetables, even the most tasteless ones, take on some character. It's picked from June to August when it is fully in bloom, in the rocky and arid areas of Calabria, Sicily, and Basilicata. I use only oregano from Aspromonte. A lady procures it for me, picking it with her children, in places that she keeps a closely guarded secret.

Preheat the oven to 350°F.

Peel the potatoes, cut them into thin slices, and place them in a bowl of cold water, then cut the tomatoes into ½-inch horizontal slices.

Lightly oil a baking sheet and then alternate the potatoes with the tomatoes, overlapping them slightly.

Season with the garlic, oregano, and salt and pepper to taste.

Drizzle some oil on top and bake until the vegetables are cooked and nicely roasted. This will take around 20 minutes.

You can also add thin slices of red onion instead of the garlic, alternated with the potatoes.

4 large potatoes
4 ripe round tomatoes
Extra-virgin olive oil
½ *garlic clove, chopped*
Wild oregano, whole leaves
Salt and freshly ground black pepper

FOR 4 PEOPLE

VEGETABLE-STUFFED
BELL PEPPERS

In traditional Southern Italian cooking, stuffed vegetables are usually filled with bread crumbs, olives, capers, and other Mediterranean herbs and spices—I've already given you some recipes. These vegetable-stuffed bell peppers are a little different, even if I wasn't able to do without the oregano and bread crumbs. Make sure you buy small vegetables so that there is the right balance between the peppers and the filling. If you prefer, you can use long peppers, such as Carmagnola peppers.

FOR 4 PEOPLE

4 small bell peppers

Salt and freshly ground black pepper

1 small eggplant

1 zucchini

1 small sweet red onion

Extra-virgin olive oil

1 ripe tomato, diced

A few basil leaves, chopped

A pinch of oregano

2 tablespoons vegan bread crumbs

Preheat the oven to 400°F.

Cut the bell peppers in two, seed them, lightly salt and pepper, and then set them aside.

Cut the eggplant, zucchini, and onion into small cubes. Heat a little oil in a small skillet. Sauté the cubed vegetables in the oil until they turn golden, then season with salt to taste.

Add the tomato to the cooked vegetables, together with the basil, oregano, and 1 tablespoon of the bread crumbs.

Mix it thoroughly, then fill the bell peppers with the stuffing and place on a baking sheet.

Dust with the remaining tablespoon of bread crumbs, then cook them in the oven until they are soft and golden brown. This should take around 25 minutes.

I've stopped suggesting it so that I don't seem obsessed, but some dried chili pepper would also go great here . . .

CAPONATA SICILIANA WITH EGGPLANT, PEPPERS, AND CAPERS

I want to go against the grain here by saying that *caponata siciliana* is not an appetizer, nor is it even a side. It was created as a main course. Actually, it's very likely that it was a full meal, as vegetable stews often were in peasant cooking. And, to all effects, it is an extremely appetizing dish that will fill you up if you accompany it with some nice, rustic bread. The eggplant in this recipe is a testament to its role as a "solid" ingredient in Southern Italian cooking and it practically replaces meat and fish during the summer. It usually takes the place of the *capone*—"gurnard"—fish (which is where the name caponata comes from), considered to be utterly exquisite and reserved for the tables of aristocrats, which common folk could not afford. This is the recipe that a Sicilian friend gave me.

Dice the eggplants into 1-inch cubes, then place them in a colander, sprinkle with coarse salt, and place a weight on top to remove the water. After an hour, squeeze them out. Heat a generous amount of oil in a large, deep skillet, and fry the eggplant cubes. Remove them when they are nicely golden and place them on paper towels to soak up the oil.

Cut the celery into small pieces, blanch them in a small pot of salted, boiling water, then blot them dry. Heat a small amount of oil in a large skillet and sauté them. Set aside.

Remove the celery from the oil and then sauté the onion in the same way. Toss in the capers and olives. Sauté them for a few minutes, then add the tomatoes and cook for around 15 minutes until the mixture reduces.

Add the eggplant and celery and season with salt to taste.

After about 10 minutes, sprinkle some sugar on the caponata and pour in the vinegar, a bit at a time, tasting as you go to get the right balance between sweet and sour. Serve cold.

You could add toasted almond flakes or serve it alongside vegan dark chocolate that you have melted in a water bath, with some freshly ground black pepper or a pinch of crushed chili pepper to add some flavor.

2 pounds oval eggplants
Coarse salt
Extra-virgin olive oil
4 celery stalks
1 onion, finely diced
2 tablespoons salted capers, rinsed thoroughly
1 cup pitted green olives, coarsely chopped
1 pound ripe tomatoes, peeled and crushed with a fork
Salt
2 tablespoons sugar
About 1 cup wine vinegar

FOR 4 PEOPLE

SPICED
STEWED CHERRIES

Cherries are mouthwatering and beautiful, like all small-fruit varieties, and they have tons of vitamins and precious substances that the body needs. This is one of those extremely rare cases where a delicious and tempting food is also good for you. Unfortunately, all that vitamin C and A won't save you from getting the unavoidable stomachache from gorging. In the neighborhood that I grew up in, just one field had survived, surrounded by apartment buildings, where there was a single cherry tree. We children just could not resist the allure of eating cherries from that tree. That's why we would climb over the gate and go and steal them, even if the farmer would catch us every so often and chase after us with a cane, most probably smiling beneath his mustache. Cooked cherries—even just with sugar—are a real delicacy. I make large quantities of them: I keep them ready in the refrigerator and put them in vegan yogurt in the morning.

FOR 4 PEOPLE

1 cup full-bodied red wine

½ cup light brown sugar

1 cinnamon stick

1 whole clove

A few black peppercorns

1 pound cherries

Boil the wine with the sugar and spices in a large pot for around 10 minutes, then toss in the cherries, with or without their pit and stem—it makes no difference.

Leave them to cook over low heat until the cherries change color and shrivel up a little. This should take around 10 minutes.

Serve them cold with their sauce, by themselves or with some good ice cream.

Durone nero di Vignola black cherries are perfect for this recipe.
You can also use almond extract or liqueur in place of the spices.

APRICOT PUDDING

Puddings are some of the easiest desserts to convert to the vegan diet. They often have a fruit base and all you need to do is replace the eggs with another binding ingredient and perhaps a little baking powder instead of the whipped egg whites. You can use all the seasonal fruit that you like. I have chosen to make the classic pudding with vegan biscotti, like those produced in Piedmont (but without using amaretti cookies, which are made with egg whites). It's outstanding at the end of a meal.

FOR 4 PEOPLE

2 pounds apricots

½ cup sugar

Fresh lemon juice

½ cup vegan biscotti, crumbled (plus a few more for the molds)

⅓ cup toasted almonds, chopped

2 tablespoons cornstarch

½ teaspoon baking powder

Vegan butter for the molds

Preheat the oven to 350°F.

Blend the apricots in a blender or food processor together with the sugar and a little lemon juice, so that they darken in color.

Mix this pulp in a large bowl with the crumbled biscuits, almonds, cornstarch, and baking powder. Stir all the ingredients together, without beating too much.

Grease four single-portion molds with the butter, sprinkle them with the reserved crumbled biscuits, and fill them no more than two-thirds full with the apricot mixture. Set in a deep baking pan large enough to hold all the molds and fill the pan halfway with water, to make a water bath.

Bake the apricot puddings in their water bath until they are nicely golden and have puffed up. This will take around 40 minutes.

You can add toasted almond flakes for decoration.

DEEP-FRIED FRUIT

You'll have to excuse me. I should be suggesting a lovely, summer fruit salad at this point—but you can always make those, even without my instructions, perhaps adding seeds, herbs, and spices that are to your liking. Unfortunately, I'm not able to stay too far from my skillet. My husband says that the Italian expression "we're fried" could be our motto. That's why even summer fruits are tossed in batter and inevitably end up in sizzling oil.

Mix the flour with the sugar in a bowl, then add enough wine and sparkling water to get a smooth batter, without stirring too much. Leave it to rest in the refrigerator for half an hour.

Choose cherries that are attached in twos on the stem, or tie them in groups of two or four. Cut the plums and apricots in two and remove the pits.

Heat a generous amount of oil in a large, deep skillet. Dip the fruit in the batter and then fry it in the hot oil until golden brown, frying the cherries first, then the apricots, and then the plums last. Dry the fried fruit on paper towels, then serve as is, or sprinkle some powdered sugar on top.

Add some flavor to the batter with cinnamon or another spice of your choice. I really like saffron.

1¼ cups all-purpose flour

1 teaspoon sugar

½ cup fruity wine

Sparkling water

16 cherries

4 plums

4 apricots

Peanut oil, for frying

Powdered sugar (optional)

FOR 6 PEOPLE

PLUM AND HAZELNUT PIE

I'm not generally a big fan of desserts, but I adore pies made with summer fruits, especially plums, which are a bit sour and therefore provide a nice contrast in this dessert. Hazelnuts go with plums better than any other kind of nut, but I've also tried using almonds, which—in addition to being delicious—are also good for you, and the pie is scrumptious all the same. For the hazelnut piecrust, follow the piecrust instructions on page 23—you just need to replace ½ cup of the flour with the same amount of toasted, ground hazelnuts, blended with a little sugar so they don't clump together.

FOR 4 PEOPLE

Vegan butter and all-purpose flour, for pan

1½ pounds Stanley plums

2 tablespoons light brown sugar

1 batch hazelnut piecrust (see headnote and Piecrust recipe, page 23)

¼ cup toasted hazelnuts, ground

Lemon zest

Preheat the oven to 350°F. Butter and flour a 10-inch pie pan.

Cut the plums in half and remove the pits, then lay them out on a parchment-lined baking sheet and sprinkle them with some brown sugar. Place them under the grill on the maximum temperature setting for around 10 minutes, until they reduce a bit in size.

Roll out the hazelnut pie dough on a lightly floured work surface and place in the prepared pie pan. Flute the edge of the pie by pinching it with your fingers, then prick the bottom with the tines of a fork.

Layer the plums on the crust, sprinkle with the remaining brown sugar, the ground hazelnuts, and the lemon zest, then place in the oven. Bake until the edges of the pie are golden brown and the plums have caramelized. This will take around 25 minutes.

Stanley plums are some of the best when it comes to cooking because they contain very little water. You can even put some fresh ones on top of the pie. If you do, spread some crumbled vegan biscotti on the bottom to absorb the extra juices.

WATERMELON ICE

In Sicily, watermelon is called *mellone*—"melon"—an abbreviation used in Southern Italy to distinguish it from *melone di pane*, the white or orange kind of melon that is simply called *melone* in the rest of Italy. I call watermelon *cocomero* if I'm in Florence, *zipangulu* if I'm in Calabria. This is the summer fruit par excellence—refreshing, hydrating, and it doesn't weigh you down if you eat it outside of meal times. Watermelon Ice is a specialty made in Palermo for Ferragosto—an Italian holiday celebrated on August 15—and throughout the entire melon harvesting season, but it's also made in other parts of Sicily with small variations.

Blend the watermelon in a blender or food processor, push it through a strainer to remove the seeds, then place it in a large pot, reserving a little of the watermelon juice.

Dissolve the cornstarch in a cup with the reserved watermelon juice and then add it, together with the sugar, to the watermelon pulp, whisking it vigorously to keep lumps from forming.

Place the pot over low heat and bring to a boil. Keep stirring with a wooden spoon for 2 minutes, then remove from the stove and leave to cool.

Add the candied pumpkin and then the chocolate chips and pistachios (keep some aside for garnish). Slightly dampen four single-portion ramekins or cups with water. Divide the watermelon mixture among the ramekins, then refrigerate them for 5 to 6 hours.

If you've used ramekins, turn out the ice onto serving plates to serve; if you've used cups, serve directly in the cups.

Garnish with the reserved chocolate chips and pistachios.

Zuccata, an ingredient in this recipe, is a kind of traditional candied pumpkin from Sicily. You can also use candied watermelon rind or any other kind of candied fruit. You can add a few tablespoons of jasmine water or use flowers for garnish.

8 cups watermelon pulp

⅔ cup cornstarch

½ cup sugar

¼ cup candied pumpkin, diced (see note)

½ cup vegan chocolate chips (70% cacao with 46% fat)

3 tablespoons toasted and chopped pistachios

FOR 4 PEOPLE

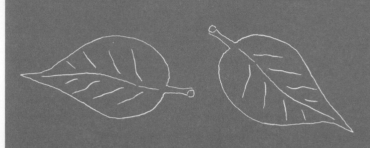

APPETIZERS

Fall Crostini, 110

Grilled Polenta with Mushrooms

with White Bean Puree and Sage

Sardinian Flatbread with Caramelized Onion
and Trevisano Radicchio

Bell Peppers with Grapes
and Rosemary, 112

Mini Escarole Calzones, 113

Orange Salad, 114

Endive, Pear, and Walnut Salad, 115

Baked Chickpea Pie with Onions, 116

Red Lentil Salad, 118

Baked Pumpkin with Herbs, 119

Leek Tart, 120

FIRST COURSES

Pumpkin and Potato Soup with
Chestnuts, 121

Leek Soup, 122

Florentine Carabaccia Soup, 124

Broccoli Rabe and Bean Soup, 125

Pumpkin Gnocchi with Sugo Finto
Vegan Ragout, 126

Mushroom and Artichoke Lasagna, 127

Fettucine with Trevisano Radicchio
and Pumpkin, 128

Chickpea Cacciucco Stew, 130

Fava Bean and Chicory Maccu Soup, 131

Spaghetti alla Carrettiera, 132

Mixed Pasta and Chickpeas, 133

FALL

MAIN COURSES

Roasted Mixed Vegetables with
Potato Puree, 134

Stuffed Baked Onions, 136

Stuffed Porcini Mushrooms, 137

Potato and Cauliflower Stew, 138

Mushroom and Potato Bake, 139

Fennel Pie, 140

Chard Balls with Gremolata, 141

DESSERTS

Focaccia with Grapes
and Rosemary, 142

Pears in Red Wine Sauce, 144

Rich Castagnaccio/Chestnut Cake, 145

Crumbly Cake with Hazelnuts, 146

Flaky Orange Cake, 147

FALL CROSTINI

It's easy to imagine these crunchy and delicious morsels as a light meal with a good glass of red wine. Polenta with mushrooms is a fall classic. Choose your favorites: chiodini, chanterelle, porcini, or white button. In Tuscany beans are often combined with sage which I've chosen to make crunchy. The Sardinian flatbread *pane carasau* is thin and fragrant and "comes" from the Barbagia area to "meet" caramelized radicchio from Treviso. This is a real gastronomic medley, but the result is fantastic.

Extra-virgin olive oil

2½ cups mixed mushrooms (chop the larger ones)

1 garlic clove, crushed

1 bunch flat-leaf parsley

Leaves from 1 sprig lesser calamint or mint (optional)

Salt and freshly ground black pepper

4 slices polenta

GRILLED POLENTA WITH MUSHROOMS

Heat a little oil in a medium skillet. Put the mushrooms, garlic, a few parsley leaves, and the lesser calamint (if using) in the pan and cook, covered, for around 15 minutes, until all the water from the mushrooms has been absorbed, then season with salt and pepper to taste. Toast the polenta in the oven or on a grill. Spread the mushroom mixture on top of the polenta and finish off with some chopped parsley.

CROSTINI WITH WHITE BEAN PUREE AND SAGE

Heat a tablespoon of oil in a small pan, then toss in the sage leaves with the garlic and fry them lightly until crunchy and golden brown. Remove the garlic and add the sage to the pureed beans, reserving a few fried leaves for garnish. Season with salt and pepper. Spread the bean puree on the slices of toast, garnish with the crunchy sage leaves, a drizzle of oil, and a sprinkle of pepper.

Extra-virgin olive oil

A few sage leaves

1 garlic clove

1 cup cooked and pureed white beans

Salt and freshly ground black pepper

4 slices vegan whole wheat bread, toasted

Extra-virgin olive oil

1 small sweet red onion, sliced

1 head Trevisano radicchio (better if a late variety), chopped

1 teaspoon light brown sugar

About 2 tablespoons red wine vinegar

Salt and freshly ground black pepper

4 slices vegan Sardinian flatbread, or matzo (about 4 ounces), broken into pieces by hand

SARDINIAN FLATBREAD WITH CARAMELIZED ONION AND TREVISANO RADICCHIO

Heat some oil in a large skillet and sauté the onion for a few minutes, then add the radicchio. Cook over high heat, stirring often, until everything is lightly fried but still crisp. This should take around 10 minutes. Add the brown sugar and vinegar, add the salt and pepper to taste, and stir thoroughly. Cook for another few minutes until the wine has evaporated and the vegetables have caramelized, then taste to see whether the level of sweet and sour is to your liking. If not, add more sugar or vinegar. Leave to cool, then spread over the Sardinian flatbread and serve.

BELL PEPPERS
WITH GRAPES AND ROSEMARY

If you can get your hands on heart-shaped peppers like the ones you still find in abundance in Calabria come the end of September, that would be perfect. They are fleshy, crunchy, and oh so fragrant, not to mention perfect for stuffing or eating raw. My Aunt Saruzza used to cut them down the side to remove the seeds and create a sort of bowl that she would season with a big pinch of salt and plenty of olive oil. She would let it drip onto a piece of bread a little, then take a bite of the bread and a bite of the pepper. For me, this was the best snack in the world. Perhaps it's because I grew up in Florence, where grapes and rosemary are the ingredients of a traditional dessert made around grape-harvesting time, and so it seemed completely natural to me to put them together and add, for flavor, a little Tropea red onion, Calabria's pride and joy. It can be replaced with sweet red onion.

FOR 4 PEOPLE

2 pounds bell peppers,
    sliced diagonally

1 sweet red onion, sliced

1 bunch white grapes

Leaves from 1 sprig rosemary

Extra-virgin olive oil

Salt and freshly ground
    black pepper

Preheat the oven to 400°F.

Put the bell pepper and onion slices and the whole grapes into a baking dish. Add the rosemary, a drizzle of oil, and salt and black pepper to taste. Mix together thoroughly with your hands so that the seasoning is distributed well, then put the pan in the oven and roast for around 20 minutes, stirring once with a wooden spoon.

The peppers should end up roasted and the grapes should still be whole.

These bell peppers are delectable cold or on bread, too. The exquisite contrast between the sweetness of the grapes and the spicy flavor of the peppers becomes all the more intense.

MINI ESCAROLE CALZONES

Try to use escarole with a deep green color: It's firmer, has much more flavor, and is better for cooking. You really want the kind that comes straight from the farmer with a willow reed tied around each one—to make sure the hearts remain white—and full of dirt and little insects from the countryside. You'd have no trouble finding them at the local market stalls in Italy, where the local farmers come every day to sell their freshly harvested vegetables. A classic Southern Italian tradition involves adding escarole to bread dough. The most famous would be focaccia from Messina, but these slightly spicy calzones are not half bad, either. Try them and let me know!

Preheat the oven to 480°F. Lightly oil a baking sheet.

First and foremost, you need to "drown" the escarole. Lightly heat oil in a large skillet, then toss in the escarole, olives, parsley, and salt and pepper to taste. Sauté over high heat until the liquids evaporate and the escarole is slightly wilted but still crunchy, then set aside.

Roll out the dough on a floured work surface until it is very thin—less than ⅛-inch thick. Cut out 8-inch disks and place some sautéed escarole in the center. Fold the disks over the vegetable mixture and seal the edges tightly, folding them over themselves a little and pressing down firmly with your fingers.

Place them on the prepared baking sheet, then bake until they are nicely browned. This will take around 20 minutes.

You can also fry these mini calzones by cutting the disks a little smaller (around 4 inches in diameter).

Extra-virgin olive oil

2 pounds escarole, chopped

A handful of pitted olives in brine, chopped

1 sprig flat-leaf parsley, chopped

Salt and freshly ground black pepper

1 batch Pizza Dough (page 20)

FOR 4 PEOPLE

ORANGE SALAD

This is nothing more than a salad with orange and fennel. Oranges are known as *portualle* in Sicily, which is where the Italian name for this dish comes from—*insalata di portualle*. Dialectal terms with the same root are also found scattered throughout other Italian regions, not just in the south. A very similar term for oranges even features in the Piedmont dialect. Tracing the etymology takes us back to the historical origins of this fruit's cultivation in the Mediterranean, where it was then exported to China by Portuguese sailors, which is where the dialectal term comes from. It's well known that citrus fruits are mouthwatering when paired with some seasoning. The example that always comes to my mind is how my grandparents would eat lemons with salt on them, to cut the sourness.

Peel the oranges, removing the rind and attempting to get rid of all the bitter fibers. Cut it first in two lengthwise and then into thin slices.

Mix the oranges in a large bowl with the fennel, spring onion, parsley, and olives.

Drizzle some oil on top and season with salt and pepper to taste, then stir well and serve.

You can also use other sweet oranges, such as navel or Valencia, as long as they are fresh and juicy.

2 blood oranges

2 fennel bulbs, thinly sliced

1 fresh spring onion, finely chopped

1 sprig flat-leaf parsley, finely chopped

A handful of olives, sliced or chopped

Extra-virgin olive oil

Salt and freshly ground black pepper

FOR 4 PEOPLE

ENDIVE, PEAR, AND WALNUT SALAD

Because it is grown in the dark, Belgian endive is white, tender, and crunchy at the same time, and is often served baked or au gratin. It is also outstanding in salads, as it is slightly bitter and goes well with fruit. The walnuts add a slightly spicy note and a good dose of vital nutrients. Nuts are often added in vegan salads as they are a great source of energy and important nutrients, minerals, and vitamins.

FOR 4 PEOPLE

4 heads Belgian endive

2 ripe Abate or Bosc pears

Juice of 1 lemon

¼ cup walnuts, chopped

A few fresh thyme leaves

Extra-virgin olive oil

*Salt and freshly ground
    black pepper*

Wash and dry the endive, then separate the leaves and cut them into uneven strips.

Wash the pears, cut them in half lengthwise, without peeling, then core and cut into thin slices and sprinkle with some lemon juice to keep them from browning.

Put the endives and pears together in a salad bowl, then add the walnuts and thyme. Drizzle with oil and season with salt and pepper to taste. Mix well and serve.

Belgian endive leaves have a beautiful shape and are quite tough, so you can use them as little edible trays to serve nicely seasoned diced vegetables and fruits.

BAKED CHICKPEA PIE WITH ONIONS

No matter what it is called from region to region, the basic recipe always comes down to water and chickpea flour, baked to a thin, often crunchy outside. In Livorno, they put it on bread and call it Five and Five, because once upon a time, bread and chickpea pie used to cost five cents each. Try this version that has a little more garnish, which makes it really flavorful. And don't forget that baked chickpea pie should be eaten piping hot.

FOR 4 PEOPLE

2 tablespoons extra-virgin olive oil, plus more for pan

About 3 cups cold water

2 cups chickpea flour

Salt

2 sweet red onions

Leaves from a few sprigs of thyme

Peanut oil, for frying and the baking pan

Freshly ground black pepper

Preheat the oven to 400°F. Lightly oil a 9-by-13 inch baking pan.

Slowly add the cold water to the chickpea flour to a mixing bowl and beat with a whisk to stop lumps from forming. Add the oil and a pinch of salt, then leave to rest for about an hour, allowing the foam that formed on the surface to dissolve.

In the meantime, peel the onions and cut them into rings. Heat oil in a medium skillet and fry them in the hot oil until they are golden brown.

Remove them with a skimmer, leave them to dry on paper towels, and then sprinkle with some salt.

Pour the chickpea flour mixture into the prepared baking pan, then layer the fried onion on top along with the thyme.

Bake the pie until it turns a nice golden color. This will take around 25 minutes.

Serve with a good sprinkle of pepper on top—it goes great.

If you want to enhance this pie even more, add some pitted olives.

RED LENTIL SALAD

Lentils are fantastic and a hit with everyone. This is partly due to their shape, which is quite nice on the palate, but also that, in Italy, people believe that they bring good fortune and wealth. They have always been considered an important legume, as attested to by the biblical story of Esau who sold his birthright to his brother for nothing more than a plate of lentils. Like all legumes, they are essential to the vegan diet due to their high protein content. These red ones don't need to be soaked and, as they have been hulled, they are very easy to digest. Most people don't think it is necessary to soak any kind of lentils for them to cook properly. I also prefer to cook them without soaking them first. I just put them in a big pot with a lot of water over low heat, perhaps with some vegetables, such as onions and carrots, to add more flavor. Mushrooms also make a regular appearance in vegan cuisine since they contain a good amount of B vitamins.

FOR 4 PEOPLE

2½ cups dried red lentils

Extra-virgin olive oil

2½ cups white button mushrooms, cleaned and sliced

1 garlic clove

Salt and freshly ground black pepper

3 cups baby spinach, washed and thoroughly dried

½ teaspoon Dijon mustard

Dried chili pepper, crushed, to taste (optional)

Cook the lentils in a large pot of salted, boiling water until they are soft but still whole, then drain.

Heat a little oil in a large skillet. Sauté the mushrooms in the oil, together with the garlic and some salt and pepper. Keep it over rather high heat, stirring often so that the mushrooms don't lose their water. Remove from the heat when still crunchy and set aside to cool.

Mix the lentils with the mushrooms and spinach in a salad bowl. Season with salt and then with a little olive oil mixed together with the mustard and a sprinkle of freshly ground pepper or, if you prefer, a pinch of dried chili pepper.

To stop the mushrooms from releasing too much water, add them to the pan two or three at a time.

BAKED PUMPKIN WITH HERBS

Usually pumpkin is sweet and a little too delicate, but when cooked this way it turns into a really delicious dish. Let's say that this recipe represents the pumpkin's other side and is nothing like the risottos made with the barucca pumpkin in the Lombardy region, or Mantuan ravioli, where the sweetness of the pumpkin is enhanced by amaretto. The recipe I'm giving you here is tasty and spicy, just as we make it in Southern Italy. It is a rich and delicious dish. You can use the classic pie pumpkin or a variety of squash such as fairytale, butternut, or long squash, which is not as sweet. Just be sure to choose the freshest herbs.

Preheat the oven to 400°F. Oil a baking sheet.

Wash and dry the pumpkin, cut it in half, remove the seeds, and then cut it into thin slices, without peeling it (especially if you are using a squash variety with a thin skin). Place the slices so that they overlap slightly on the prepared baking sheet.

Chop the herbs together with the garlic, mix them together in a bowl with the bread crumbs and chili pepper, then spread the mixture over the pumpkin.

Drizzle some oil on top and season with salt and pepper to taste.

Bake the pumpkin slices until they turn golden and crunchy on the edges. This should take around 25 minutes.

You can also replace the pumpkin with thin slices of potato.

Extra-virgin olive oil

2 pounds pumpkin

Mixed herbs: rosemary, sage, thyme, parsley

1 garlic clove

⅓ cup stale vegan bread crumbs

Dried chili pepper, crushed, to taste

Salt and freshly ground black pepper

FOR 4 PEOPLE

LEEK TART

Finally, we are about to use a vegan substitute recipe! That would be béchamel made with vegan butter and soy or rice milk. I have to say that it's not half bad. It still has a nice consistency and great flavor, even without real butter and cow's milk. You can find ready-made vegan puff pastry in supermarkets, or you can make it, following the steps in the basic recipe section of this book.

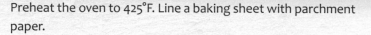

FOR 4 PEOPLE

3 leeks

Extra-virgin olive oil

Salt

1 roll ready-made vegan puff pastry or ½ pound homemade (page 22)

1 batch Béchamel Sauce (page 18)

Freshly grated nutmeg

Freshly ground black pepper

A small piece of vegan butter

Preheat the oven to 425°F. Line a baking sheet with parchment paper.

Cut the leeks into thin rounds, including the green tops. Heat a little oil in a medium skillet. Sauté the leeks in the oil until they soften, then season with salt and set aside.

Roll out the puff pastry on the prepared baking sheet, prick it with the tines of a fork, then layer the leeks on top and cover with the béchamel sauce. Fold the sides of the dough over a little to create a decorative edge.

Finish off with some nutmeg, pepper, and a few shavings of butter, then bake until the tart has puffed up and is golden brown. This should take about 30 minutes.

You can also use other seasonal vegetables, such as fennel, cauliflower, or carrots.

PUMPKIN AND POTATO SOUP WITH CHESTNUTS

This is a Northern Italian dish from Venetian cuisine with a light note of Tuscany provided by the "charred" chestnuts that provide the garnish and the extra-virgin olive oil added just before serving. In my native Calabria, pumpkin (*zucca*) is called *cucuzza*, and used to be grown and mixed with leftovers as food for the pigs. Today it's quite popular all over the place. Whole pumpkins keep for months on end, as long as the skin is intact and the stem firmly attached. When I harvest them from my garden, I leave them on the sideboard because they are so lovely to look at—even up until Christmas. When I do finally decide to cook them, they are always wonderful and tasty.

Cut the leek into rounds, including the green tops. Heat a little oil in a large skillet. Fry the leeks lightly in the oil with a pinch of salt, then cook, covered, over medium heat for around 10 minutes.

Add the potato and pumpkin, leave to develop more flavor for a few minutes, then add the hot water.

Preheat the oven to 400°F.

Season with salt and pepper, bring to boil, then leave to cook, covered, over low heat until the vegetables are almost overcooked and the liquid has evaporated a little. This should take around 30 minutes.

In the meantime, notch an X into the chestnuts with a knife and roast them in the oven until they are soft on the inside and a little roasted on the outside.

Use an immersion blender to puree the soup together with the vegan cream—if you plan on adding it—then bring to boil and remove from the heat.

Pour the pumpkin soup onto four bowls. Garnish with the shelled and chopped roasted chestnuts and a drizzle of oil, then serve.

In Tuscany, they call roasted chestnuts *bruciate*, meaning "charred" and they pronounce it with a heavily aspirated *c* (a *sh* sound). Boiled chestnuts with wild fennel, on the other hand, are called *ballotte*—"shot."

1 leek

Extra-virgin olive oil

Salt

1 large potato, diced

1¼ pounds pumpkin or squash, peeled and diced (Long of Naples, butternut, or fairytale variety)

1 quart hot water

Freshly ground black pepper

About 10 chestnuts

2 tablespoons vegan cream (optional)

FOR 4 PEOPLE

LEEK SOUP

Pureed soups are a great thing—they warm you up, they comfort you, and they help you get through those tedious, gray fall days. Personally speaking, I prefer to spice things up a little with a good dose of my own chili pepper, sun dried and then ground just enough so as to crush the seeds. I've added some toasted seeds in this recipe, not because they're fashionable, but because they're rich in calcium and other valuable substances—an excellent supplement for people following a vegan diet.

FOR 4 PEOPLE

3 leeks

Extra-virgin olive oil

Salt and freshly ground
    black pepper

3 large potatoes, diced

1 quart hot water

2 tablespoons mixed
    toasted seeds

Dried chili pepper, crushed,
    to taste (optional)

Cut the leeks into rounds (including the green tops) and keep some aside for garnish. Sweat them in a large pot with a little oil and a pinch of salt and pepper, then lower the heat and cook, covered, for around 10 minutes.

Add the potatoes, allow them to develop some flavor for a few minutes, then add the hot water, season with salt, and bring to a boil. Simmer until the vegetables are nearly overcooked, 20 to 25 minutes, then puree with an immersion blender.

Heat a little oil in a small pan. Sauté the reserved leeks in the oil until they are golden brown.

Serve the soup garnished with the sautéed leeks, the seeds, a pinch of chili pepper—if desired—and a drizzle of oil.

Just as with the pumpkin soup in the previous recipe, you can add 2 tablespoons of vegan cream when you are blending this soup to get a more even puree.

FLORENTINE CARABACCIA SOUP

As Aldo Santini says in his book *La cucina fiorentina* (Florentine Cuisine), "Onion soup is ours and God help anyone who touches it!" Florentine Carabaccia is the precursor to the nobler and much praised *soupe aux oignons*, otherwise known as French onion soup, which arrived in France with Catherine de Médicis, who would teach the French to eat with a fork, as well as various other things concerning the gastronomic arts. The Renaissance recipe that I'm giving you here includes sugar and cinnamon, which you are free to leave out if sweetness is not your thing.

FOR 4 PEOPLE

Extra-virgin olive oil

2 pounds red onions, sliced

Salt

¾ cup chopped almonds

Ground cinnamon

1 tablespoon light brown sugar

White wine vinegar

4 cups Vegetable Stock (page 17)

4 slices vegan rustic bread, toasted

Freshly ground black pepper

Heat 4 to 5 tablespoons of oil in a large pot. If you have a terra-cotta pot, all the better. Sauté the onions in the oil with a little salt. Cover and cook until the onions are nearly transparent, then add the almonds, cinnamon, brown sugar, and 1 to 2 tablespoons of vinegar, and then stir well until the onions develop a richer flavor.

Taste to check the balance between sweet and sour and then add a little more sugar or vinegar to correct.

Add the stock, season with salt to taste, then bring to a boil. Lower the heat and leave to cook, covered, for around half an hour.

Place the toasted bread in shallow bowls, pour the onion soup on top, and serve with a sprinkling of pepper.

If you don't want to use sugar or cinnamon, you'll have to omit the vinegar, too. If you decide to use ramekins instead of bowls, you can put the soup in a 400°F oven to brown for a few minutes.

BROCCOLI RABE AND BEAN SOUP

The original recipe that my grandmother and mom used to make simply called for boiling the vegetables together with the pasta, while the beans were cooked separately, and the two were then mixed together. The only added flavor came from the chili pepper and olive oil from Southern Italy, which provided its distinctive taste. In the Calabrian dialect, this kind of soup is called *mangiari maritatu*—"married foods"—because the vegetables, beans, and pasta are cooked together. If there were any leftovers, they would make a sort of *ribollita*, a Tuscan-style soup with stale bread boiled in a little water. This is a real delicacy—known as *panata*—"bread soup"—which was traditionally eaten for breakfast with a drizzle of oil.

Put the beans in a large pot with the cold water, tomato, one of the garlic cloves, and the celery and parsley. Bring to a boil, then lower the heat to the lowest setting and leave to simmer, covered, for around 2 hours, adding salt when the beans are almost cooked.

Blanch the broccoli rabe in a large pot of salted, boiling water and, when it is half done (3 to 4 minutes), add the spaghetti, broken in two. Drain it all when the pasta is cooked and add the beans with a small amount of their liquid.

Crush the remaining garlic clove. Heat a little oil in a small pan. Sauté the crushed garlic in the oil, then add it to the pot of soup.

Bring to a boil to pull all the flavors together, season with salt, and add water if the consistency is too thick.

Heat the chili pepper over a flame until it blackens, then crumble it.

Serve the soup with a drizzle of oil and the crumbled chili pepper.

You can flavor this soup even more by adding other vegetables: turnips, escarole, Swiss chard, or even wild greens.

1 cup white beans, soaked
1 quart cold water
1 tomato
2 garlic cloves
1 small celery stalk, diced
1 sprig parsley, roughly chopped
Salt
2 pounds broccoli rabe
½ pound spaghetti
Extra-virgin olive oil
1 dried chili pepper

FOR 4 PEOPLE

PUMPKIN GNOCCHI WITH SUGO FINTO VEGAN RAGOUT

Really delicious gnocchi, the ones that are still firm after cooking, yet melt in your mouth when you eat them, are already vegan—eggs are never added to gnocchi! That means it's all down to how the pumpkin is cooked; the quality of the potatoes, which should be mealy; and using just the right amount of flour. *Sugo finto* is a classic Tuscan meatless ragout; however, here the tomato has been omitted.

FOR 4 PEOPLE

For the gnocchi

2 pounds pumpkin or heritage heirloom winter squash, peeled

2 pounds white potatoes

About 1¾ cups all-purpose flour

Salt

For the sauce

4 to 5 tablespoons extra-virgin olive oil

4 ounces dried porcini mushrooms, soaked and chopped

A few sage leaves

Leaves from 1 sprig rosemary

Leaves from 1 sprig flat-leaf parsley

1 garlic clove, crushed

1 large sweet red onion, diced

1 carrot, diced

2 celery stalks, diced

Salt

½ cup white wine

Freshly ground black pepper

Preheat the oven to 425°F.

Prepare the gnocchi: Cut the pumpkin into 1-inch slices, then put them on a baking sheet and roast in the oven for around 30 minutes, until they soften. Boil the potatoes in a pot on the stovetop.

Use a potato ricer to puree the two vegetables and then mix them together, discarding the pumpkin skin. Start incorporating the flour, adding it little by little until the dough is soft but no longer sticky.

Prepare the sauce: Heat 4 to 5 tablespoons of oil in a large skillet. Combine the mushrooms, herbs, garlic, onion, carrot, celery, and a pinch of salt in the skillet and leave to sweat over low heat.

Add the white wine and cook for a further 20 minutes, adding hot water, if necessary. Season with salt and pepper to taste.

Add the pumpkin and potato gnocchi dough by the spoonful, a few at a time, to a large pot that contains a generous amount of salted, boiling water. Remove them with a skimmer as soon as they begin to float and add to the skillet of sauce.

Heat the gnocchi over high heat for a few minutes, moving the skillet so that they soak up the flavor of the sauce, then serve.

This tasty sauce is fantastic with any kind of pasta!

MUSHROOM AND ARTICHOKE LASAGNE

This isn't classic lasagne because I don't use béchamel sauce. I layer the lasagna sheets with loads of mushrooms and artichokes, pop them in the oven, and wait for them to turn the right color. That's why the lasagna sheets are only blanched slightly in boiling water and the vegetables should keep a bit of their juices, so that the pasta cooks completely and stays soft. After all, the use of béchamel—traditionally found in Bolognese lasagne and the cuisine of Emilia-Romagna in general—is lost entirely as you move farther south.

Preheat the oven to 400°F.

In a large pot, blanch the lasagna sheets in a generous amount of salted, boiling water, remove them with a skimmer, and leave to dry on a cotton cloth.

Sweat the onion and half of the garlic in a large skillet with a little oil for a few minutes, then add the mushrooms, half of the parsley, and salt and pepper. Cook for around 15 minutes without letting it reduce too much, adding warm water, if necessary.

Clean the artichokes, removing the outer leaves and tips, then cut them into thin slices.

Heat some oil in a large skillet. Sauté the artichoke slices with the remaining crushed garlic, a pinch of marjoram, remaining parsley, and a little water. Season with salt and pepper and cook until they are soft, but still moist.

Coat the bottom of a 9-by-13-inch baking pan with some of the vegetable juices, and layer the lasagna sheets, alternating with the mushroom and artichokes sauces.

Sprinkle a little bread crumbs on top and bake until golden brown, 20 to 30 minutes.

The vegetable pairing for this lasagne dish can be changed; for example, pumpkin or winter squash and radicchio, leek and celery, or carrot and fennel.

⅔ pound lasagna sheets (page 22)

Salt

1 onion, sliced

2 garlic cloves, crushed

Extra-virgin olive oil

5 cups mixed mushrooms, sliced

1 sprig flat-leaf parsley, chopped

Freshly ground black pepper

6 artichokes

Fresh marjoram

Vegan bread crumbs, for dusting

FOR 4 PEOPLE

FETTUCCINE WITH TREVISANO RADICCHIO AND PUMPKIN

For this recipe I've used late-season radicchio from Treviso, which has long, tapered leaves and is grown according to extremely stringent standards in a small strip of towns in the Veneto region. You can use other types of red radicchio, such as early Trevisano or the red radicchio from Verona. They are not as delicate, are slightly more bitter, and tend to release a lot of water, but they still work well. This recipe is exquisite and can be made in no time at all.

FOR 4 PEOPLE

1 pound pumpkin or winter squash (Long of Naples, butternut, or fairytale variety)

Extra-virgin olive oil

2 large heads late-variety Trevisano or red radicchio

Salt and freshly ground black pepper

⅔ cup fettuccine pasta

Leaves from 1 sprig flat-leaf parsley

Peel the pumpkin and cut the flesh into slices, making sure that they are not too thin or uneven. Heat a little oil in a medium skillet. Cook the pumpkin slices in the oil over high heat, stirring occasionally with a wooden spoon, for around 15 minutes. You'll see that some of the pumpkin will still be intact and a little carmelized, while the thinner part will crumble a little.

Clean the radicchio and cut it at the roots, so that the leaves come apart (or, if you prefer, you can cut it into pieces). Heat some oil in a large skillet. Add the radicchio to the oil, adding salt and pepper to taste. Cook over high heat, stirring every so often, until the radicchio has browned but is still crunchy. This should take around 15 minutes.

Add the cooked pumpkin, season with salt and pepper to taste, and cook for another few minutes to blend the flavors.

Cook the fettuccine al dente in a large pot of salted water, then (reserving the pasta water) remove it with a skimmer and put it into the pan of vegetables.

Cook it all over high heat for a few minutes, then add a little of the pasta water, if necessary. Finish off with a few parsley leaves and some pepper and serve.

If you like, add half of a sweet red onion, sliced, to the pan along with the radicchio. Late-season radicchio is also excellent raw, dressed in a salad with white beans.

CHICKPEA CACCIUCCO STEW

This has nothing in common with the Livorno *cacciucco*, a fish stew, but is just as delicious and nutritious, too. It is a traditional Tuscan dish made with Swiss chard, and sometimes seasonal wild greens are tossed in as well. The traditional recipe calls for a salted anchovy to be dissolved in the cooking oil. Of course I've not done this and I have to say that this cacciucco is even more tasty for it. Chickpeas have a strong flavor that satisfies the palate and they don't need a lot of seasoning.

FOR 4 PEOPLE

Extra-virgin olive oil

1 sweet red onion, diced

2 garlic cloves, (1 crushed, 1 left whole)

¾ pound Swiss chard, roughly chopped

1 pound tomatoes, peeled

Salt and freshly ground black pepper

3 cups chickpeas, cooked

3 slices vegan rustic bread, toasted

Heat 3 to 4 tablespoons of oil in a large pot and sauté the onion and the crushed garlic. Toss in the Swiss chard and lightly fry it for a few minutes.

Add the tomatoes, stir, season with salt and pepper and cook for around 20 minutes. Add some warm water if the Swiss chard has not released enough juices while cooking.

Add the chickpeas, making sure that there is enough liquid to moisten the bread; otherwise, add a few ladles of warm water. Simmer over low heat for another 10 minutes to let it develop a deeper flavor.

Rub the remaining garlic clove over the bread slices, then place them in four bowls and pour the stew over the bread.

Serve this Chickpea Cacciucco piping hot.

If you prefer a creamier, thicker cacciucco, blend one-third of the chickpeas before adding them to the vegetables.

FAVA BEAN AND CHICORY MACCU SOUP

Dried bean *maccu*—a thick, bean-based soup—is made with pasta in Calabria, whereas they add wild fennel in Sicily to give it flavor. However, I think that the region that does it best is Apulia, which pairs it with chicory. This creates an extremely appealing flavor contrast, as the chicory keeps its bitterness, while the fava beans are sweet and soft. Apulian cuisine has a special fondness for wild herbs, such as the wild chicory found in this recipe. However, if you're not a fan of going out into the fields to pick herbs, puntarelle will go great, too.

Soak the fava beans for 12 hours in a bowl filled with a lot of cold water.

Drain them, then put them in a large pot with the onion, cover with cold water, and bring to simmer. Cook until they are quite soft, about 30 minutes, adding warm water, if necessary.

Season with salt and beat with a wooden spoon, adding the oil a little at a time, until the beans have become a rough puree.

Blanch the wild chicory in a pot of salted, boiling water.

Serve the maccu with the chicory and a drizzle of oil on top. Some ground pepper or a pinch of chili pepper would not be bad, either.

When cooking the fava beans, use just enough water to cover them, otherwise the maccu will be too watery.

FOR 4 PEOPLE

2 cups dried fava beans, shelled

½ sweet red onion, diced

Cold water

Salt

Extra-virgin olive oil

2 pounds wild chicory or puntarelle

Freshly ground black pepper or dried chili pepper, crushed, to taste (optional)

SPAGHETTI ALLA CARRETTIERA

This is the recipe that is best known in the central-southern regions of Italy, Tuscany included. However, the original version comes from eastern Sicily, from the province of Ragusa, to be exact, and is actually something else entirely—in fact, the spaghetti is dressed with raw garlic, oil, pecorino cheese, and chili pepper. Tradition has it that it was invented by *carrettieri*— carters—who took just enough food with them as needed to make their meals, with mostly nonperishable ingredients. I have of course done away with the pecorino cheese!

FOR 4 PEOPLE

1 bunch flat-leaf parsley

4 garlic cloves

Extra-virgin olive oil

Dried chili pepper, finely chopped, to taste

1 pound tomatoes, peeled and crushed

Salt and freshly ground black pepper

1 pound spaghetti

Chop most of the parsley with all of the garlic. Heat 3 to 4 tablespoons of oil in a large skillet over low heat. Brown the garlic mixture, along with the chili pepper, in the oil.

Remove it from the heat for a second, otherwise it will burn, and add the tomatoes, season with salt and pepper to taste, and then put it back on the heat, stirring every so often, until the oil starts to float to the surface. This should take around 20 minutes.

Cook the pasta al dente in a large pot of salted water, drain it, and toss it into the pan of sauce. Cook it over high heat for a few minutes, then serve it with the remaining chopped parsley sprinkled on top.

A tablespoon of nutritional yeast flakes would also be a nice addition to add flavor and a bit of crunchiness.

MIXED PASTA AND CHICKPEAS

In Calabria they used to make pasta and chickpeas for the needy on March 19, the feast day of St. Joseph. My grandmother would tell me how they used to cook it on a wood-burning stove, in huge pots set up outside, using the various shapes of whatever pasta happened to be left in the pantry, as well as chickpeas. The younger girls in the town, the "maidens," would go house to house, giving it out, and would get a small gift in return. This custom of sharing pasta and chickpeas between neighbors in honor of the saint still survives to this day.

Soak the chickpeas in a bowl of cold water for 12 hours, then drain them and put them in a large pot, covered with more cold water, together with the celery, onion, garlic, tomatoes, and a drizzle of oil.

Leave them simmering, covered, until they are soft, adding the salt when they are almost cooked.

Cook the pasta and drain when it is half-cooked, then add it to the pot of chickpeas and cook for another 5 minutes, adding a few ladlefuls of warm water, if necessary. Don't let it reduce too much—it should still be somewhat liquid.

Serve the pasta and chickpeas with a drizzle of oil and sprinkle some pepper on top.

Usually a hodgepodge of broken spaghetti, mafaldine, penne, lumache, ditali, and linguine pastas are used in this soup. However, you can use just one kind of pasta—reginelle tube pasta, for example—and add a sprig of rosemary for a little flavor to the chickpeas.

2½ cups dried chickpeas

1 celery stalk, diced

1 small onion, diced

1 garlic clove, crushed

½ cup tomatoes, peeled

Extra-virgin olive oil

Salt and freshly ground black pepper

½ pound mixed pasta, both short and long varieties (long pasta broken in two)

FOR 4 PEOPLE

ROASTED MIXED VEGETABLES WITH POTATO PUREE

This is a lovely potato puree with olive oil and rosemary topped with oven-roasted seasonal vegetables that are nicely baked and bursting with flavor. Choose your favorite vegetables and add the herbs you like the most. However, use white potatoes, as the puree will turn out fluffier.

FOR 4 PEOPLE

Extra-virgin olive oil

2 fennel bulbs

2 heads Trevisano or red radicchio

1 pound pumpkin or winter squash

¼ savoy cabbage

2 sweet red onions

Salt and freshly ground black pepper

4 white potatoes

Leaves from 1 sprig rosemary, chopped

Preheat the oven to 400°F. Lightly oil a baking sheet.

Arrange the vegetables on the prepared baking sheet in one layer—cut the fennel into four slices each, slice the radicchio heads in two, cut the pumpkin and savoy cabbage into ½-inch slices, and halve the onions. Season with salt, pepper, and a drizzle of oil, then roast in the oven until all the vegetables are soft and browned, about 25 minutes. Turn them over once, if needed.

Peel and dice the potatoes, place them in a large pot, and then add just enough water to cover them. Cook until you can pierce them with a fork.

Drain the potatoes and put them back in the same pot, adding salt and pepper and whipping with a whisk, adding oil little by little, until they have puffed up. Add most of the rosemary and stir.

Put the puree on a serving plate and layer the roasted vegetables on top, drizzled with their own juices.

Finish it all off with a generous sprinkle of chopped rosemary and pepper.

If you want, you can even add a little soy milk when you are whipping the potato puree.

STUFFED BAKED ONIONS

The most famous stuffed onion recipe in Italy has to be the Piedmont version. However, it is in no way vegan, as meat is one of the ingredients in the stuffing. The recipe that I'm giving you here is my favorite, with very little stuffing and a lot of flavor.

FOR 4 PEOPLE

4 medium yellow onions

Salt

4 ounces dried mushrooms, soaked

Extra-virgin olive oil

1 garlic clove, chopped

1 sprig flat-leaf parsley, chopped

½ cup stale vegan bread crumbs

Freshly ground black pepper

Peel the onions, put them in a pot with a generous amount of salted, boiling water, and simmer for about 15 minutes, then remove them and set aside to cool.

Cut them horizontally, then hollow out the center to make space for the stuffing, setting aside the pulp.

Chop the soaked mushrooms. Heat a little oil in a large skillet. Sauté the mushrooms, garlic, and parsley in the oil. Add the chopped onion pulp, the bread crumbs, and salt and pepper to taste, and then cook for a few minutes to develop a deeper flavor.

Stuff the onions with this mixture, then place them in a baking pan with a little oil and ½ cup of water. Season with salt and pepper, drizzle some oil on top, and then bake until they are golden brown. This should take around 20 minutes.

These are also delicious cold. A Southern Italian twist on this recipe uses sweet red onions stuffed with bread crumbs, olives, and capers.

STUFFED PORCINI MUSHROOMS

Saying that these are stuffed is a bit of a stretch because only garlic and parsley are added with the chopped stems to these porcini caps, so as to not compromise the flavor or lose the aroma of such a fine mushroom. Another way to enjoy the flavor of these mushroom caps is to grill them with just a drizzle of oil and some freshly ground pepper.

Preheat the oven to 400°F. Lightly oil a baking pan.

Remove the mushroom stems, roughly chopping them. Heat some oil in a large skillet. Sauté the mushroom stems in the oil, together with the garlic, some of the parsley, and salt and pepper to taste.

Place the mushroom caps, bottom up, in the prepared baking pan. Place the chopped stems on top, season with salt and pepper, a drizzle of oil, and a sprinkle of bread crumbs, then bake for around 10 minutes.

Serve hot, with some parsley on top.

You can also use portobello mushroom caps, which are delicious and fleshy. You just have to increase the cooking time a little.

Extra-virgin olive oil
4 porcini mushrooms, cleaned
1 garlic clove
Leaves from 1 sprig flat-leaf parsley, chopped
Salt and freshly ground black pepper
Vegan bread crumbs

FOR 4 PEOPLE

POTATO AND CAULIFLOWER STEW

Potatoes, stewed with other vegetables to give flavor and consistency to the dish, are a staple of peasant cooking, often taking the place of a main meal. I have to say that I have never considered them to be a side dish, more a main course, and that is the kind of recipe that I am giving you here. Of course, you could use other vegetables instead of cauliflower, just as long as they are very flavorful, such as broccoli or artichokes. You could also try combining potatoes with tomatoes, eggplant, or bell peppers during the summer—or even mix them all together.

FOR 4 PEOPLE

4 large, yellow potatoes, peeled and diced

1 small cauliflower, separated into florets

1 sweet red onion, sliced

1 garlic clove, crushed

3 to 4 tablespoons tomato sauce

Dried chili pepper, finely chopped, to taste

Salt and freshly ground black pepper

Extra-virgin olive oil

Place the potatoes, cauliflower, onion, garlic, tomato sauce, chili pepper, salt, and black pepper in a large pot. Drizzle with 3 to 4 tablespoons of oil, then add 1 inch of warm water.

Cook, covered, for around 25 minutes, until the vegetables are tender, making sure to move the pot every so often so that the vegetables don't stick to the bottom, yet not actually stirring so as not to break them up.

Serve with a drizzle of oil on top.

Since we're on the subject of potatoes, I just have to give you this other simple recipe too! Peel the potatoes and cut them into large chunks. Notch each piece horizontally and slip a dampened, salted sage leaf into each space. Fry them in a good amount of boiling oil until they are golden brown and thoroughly cooked. They are fantastic!

MUSHROOM AND POTATO BAKE

The kind of mushroom called for in this recipe is called *cardoncelli*, as they grow together with thistles, which are known as *cardi* in Italian. They grow wild in many Southern Italian regions, but the best are found in the Murge area, a plateau located in an extremely picturesque area of Apulia. In English, you would call them king oyster mushrooms. This variety has a very delicate taste and a lovely, meaty texture, which makes it extremely versatile when it comes to cooking. They go great with other vegetables; are outstanding sautéed, baked, or stewed; and are perfect for preserving in oil and served as an appetizer.

Preheat the oven to 400°F. Lightly oil a baking pan.

Cut both the onion and potatoes into thin slices. Cut the mushrooms lengthwise into slightly thicker slices. Chop the garlic and parsley together.

Layer the vegetables into the prepared pan, alternating the onion, potatoes, and mushrooms. Dress every layer with the parsley mixture, a drizzle of oil, and some salt and pepper.

Finish it off with a sprinkle of bread crumbs and then drizzle some more oil and ½ cup of water on top.

Bake until the vegetables are soft (when they're cooked, you'll be able to pierce them easily with a fork) and golden brown. This should take around 25 minutes.

If you can't find king oyster mushrooms, the recipe will work just as well with porcini mushrooms.

Extra-virgin olive oil
1 large onion
1 pound potatoes
1 pound king oyster mushrooms, cleaned
2 garlic cloves
1 bunch flat-leaf parsley
Salt and freshly ground black pepper
Vegan bread crumbs, for sprinkling

FOR 4 PEOPLE

FENNEL PIE

This can be an extremely labor-intensive recipe—some people blanch the fennel before flouring it, frying it, and then baking it with the béchamel sauce to brown. That's a lot of work and you further run the risk of losing the distinctive flavor of the fennel. That's why I'm giving you a simpler version, yet one that is quite tasty, with chopped almonds and hazelnuts added to give some crunchiness to the pie as well as a good dose of nutrients. Sometimes I don't even add béchamel—just a sprinkle of bread crumbs and then straight into the oven!

FOR 4 PEOPLE

4 large fennel bulbs,
   cleaned and trimmed

Extra-virgin olive oil

Salt and freshly ground
   black pepper

1 batch Béchamel
   Sauce (page 18)

¼ cup mixed hazelnuts and
   almonds, coarsely chopped

Vegan bread crumbs
   for garnish

Cut the fennel in half and then into ½-inch slices. Heat a little oil in a large skillet. Sauté the fennel in the oil with a little water, over high heat, until it has absorbed the liquid and is still crunchy but browned. Only then should you season with salt and pepper.

Spread a little of the béchamel sauce on the bottom of a 9-by-13-inch baking dish, then arrange the fennel into a single layer and cover it with the béchamel.

Spread the chopped almonds and hazelnuts over the entire surface, then sprinkle with some bread crumbs. Bake until the pie is golden brown. This will take 20 to 30 minutes.

You might also add a few curls of vegan butter before you put it in the oven, though it's not essential.

CHARD BALLS WITH GREMOLATA

The idea for this recipe came to me when I was thinking about a particular kind of fritter that my grandmother used to make, very similar to the recipes that I gave you in the spring recipes section. She would make them with the hard stems of Swiss chard, which she called *secari*, as they are called in the Calabrian dialect. I've added potatoes to give the mixture some texture to enable you to shape the balls. The gremolata is indeed the traditional topping used in Milanese cuisine, which I'm giving you in a sage and rosemary version.

Boil the potatoes, then peel and mash them.

Blanch the Swiss chard in a large pot of salted water, then drain and squeeze out any excess water. Chop the chard roughly. Mix the chard with the potatoes, olives, half of the garlic, a little parsley, and some salt and pepper.

Stir well to get an even mixture, then shape into balls just a little bigger than a walnut and roll them in the flour.

Heat a little oil in a large, deep skillet. Brown the balls in the oil, then add the tomato sauce and an inch of warm water. Season with salt and pepper and leave it to reduce, moving the pan every so often to turn the balls.

To make the gremolata, chop the remaining garlic, sage, rosemary, and lemon zest together.

Add the gremolata to the balls and cook them for another 2 minutes, moving the pan so that they develop a deeper flavor.

The same potato and Swiss chard mixture can be rolled in bread crumbs and fried in oil to make croquettes.

2 large potatoes
1 pound Swiss chard
Salt
A handful of pitted olives, chopped
1 garlic clove, chopped
Leaves from 1 sprig flat-leaf parsley
Freshly ground black pepper
¾ cup all-purpose flour
Extra-virgin olive oil
¾ cup tomato sauce
A few sage leaves
Leaves from 1 sprig rosemary
Zest of 1 lemon

FOR 4 PEOPLE

FOCACCIA
WITH GRAPES AND ROSEMARY

This is not the traditional recipe for the focaccia that you find at every bakery and patisserie in Florence during grape harvest time, made with wine grapes—usually the red Canaiolo variety. This recipe only includes one layer and can be made with any kind of grape you have at hand, white or red. It's not actually a dessert, because it's not very sweet. In fact, the dough is savory. . . . However, I'd say it always goes down like a treat; you just need to be hungry!

FOR 4 PEOPLE

Extra-virgin olive oil
1 batch Pizza Dough (page 20)
2 pounds white or red grapes
½ cup light brown sugar
Leaves from 1 sprig rosemary
Freshly ground black pepper

Preheat the oven to 450°F. Lightly oil a 10-by-15-inch baking sheet, then use your hands to stretch out the pizza dough on the prepared baking sheet.

Lightly crush the grapes in a bowl, then mix them with half of the brown sugar. Spread them over the dough, then press down with your fingers so that they go into the dough a little. Cover the baking sheet with a cotton cloth and leave to rest for half an hour, so that the dough has time to rise again.

Sprinkle the focaccia with the remaining brown sugar, garnish with a few rosemary leaves (if you can find it with flowers, you can also add those once it has baked), and top it with some pepper. Bake until the dough turns golden brown. This will take around 25 minutes.

They call rosemary *ramerino* in Florence. It is the crucial ingredient in another traditional dessert made with bread dough, typically on Holy Thursday: *pan di ramerino*—rosemary and raisin buns.

PEARS
IN RED WINE SAUCE

Within the Langhe area, it's traditional to use Martin Sec pears when making this dessert. They are small, with a firm, fragrant flesh, but are really difficult to find outside of Piedmont. Thus you can also use Bosc or similar pears instead. The wine should be full-bodied, such as Dolcetto or Barbera wines, if you want to avoid the more classic and noble Barolo. I prefer to add orange zest for flavor, but you can also use lemon zest.

FOR 4 PEOPLE

4 firm, ripe pears

1¾ cups full-bodied red wine

2¼ cups light brown sugar

Some orange or lemon zest

A few whole cloves

1 cinnamon stick

Stand the washed and dried pears, tightly packed, in a high-sided saucepan.

Pour the wine over them and add all the other ingredients, then cook them, covered, over low heat, until you can pierce them with a toothpick. This should take around 35 minutes.

Remove them from the pan and thicken the cooking juices over high heat.

Serve the pears with their juices drizzled over the top. They are delicious hot, as well as cold.

If you prefer, you can bake the pears in the oven at 400°F. This will take around 1 hour.

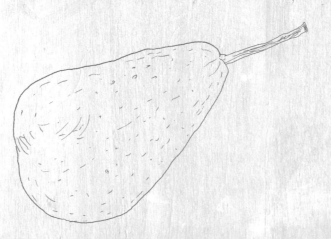

RICH CASTAGNACCIO/ CHESTNUT CAKE

If I'm being completely honest, I've never been particularly fond of the traditional recipe for this dessert that is so popular in Tuscany (I think I'm right in saying it was invented in Lucca) and which can be found throughout the Apennine areas of various Italian regions, all the way down to Lazio. It is already a vegan recipe, consisting of just chestnut flour, water, olive oil, pine nuts, rosemary, and other occasional additions, such as raisins and orange zest. Pellegrino Artusi—best known as the author of *The Science of Cooking and the Art of Fine Dining*—calls his recipe "Migliaccio with sweet flour"; he doesn't even add any sugar. I've always added some to "soften" it a little and I don't think the outcome is half bad.

Preheat the oven to 350°F. Lightly oil a 10-inch baking pan.

Sift the chestnut flour with the cocoa powder and a pinch of salt into a mixing bowl, then add 2 tablespoons of the brown sugar and gradually add the water, beating with a whisk so that lumps don't form.

Add 3 tablespoons of olive oil, the orange zest, and two-thirds of the hazelnuts and raisins. You should get a slightly runny mixture.

Pour the mixture into the prepared baking pan. Arrange the pear slices and the remaining hazelnuts and raisins over the mixture, then finish with the soaked rosemary leaves.

Sprinkle the remaining brown sugar over the top, then bake until a nice crust forms on the surface and the cake is firm on the inside but not too dry. This should take around 45 minutes.

Castagnaccio should never be too high, so be careful when choosing the size of your cake pan. These proportions are for a 10-inch pan.

3 tablespoons extra-virgin olive oil, plus more for pan

2⅓ cups chestnut flour

2 tablespoons unsweetened cocoa powder

Salt

3 tablespoons light brown sugar

About 2 cups cold water

Zest of 1 orange

A small handful of toasted, crushed hazelnuts

¼ cup raisins, soaked and drained

1 small, firm pear, peeled, cored, and thinly sliced

Leaves from 1 sprig rosemary, soaked and drained

FOR 6 PEOPLE

CRUMBLY CAKE WITH HAZELNUTS

This is a traditional dessert from Mantua and let's just say that it presents a real challenge for a vegan cookbook, as the original crumbly cake is made with nothing less than lard. Over time almonds have replaced hazelnuts in our family's day-to-day use. I've replaced the lard or butter with organic sunflower oil margarine.

FOR 8 PEOPLE

1⅓ cups toasted hazelnuts

¾ cup sugar

1¾ cups cake flour (Italian "type 00" flour), plus more for pan

1⅔ cups yellow cornmeal, such as Fioretto

Salt

Zest of 1 lemon

½ pound (2 sticks) vegan butter, chilled

2 to 3 tablespoons cold fruity white wine or water

Extra-virgin olive oil, for pan

Crush the hazelnuts together with the sugar, then mix in a large bowl with the flour and the cornmeal, a pinch of salt and the lemon zest. Cut the chilled butter into pieces and incorporate them into the flour with your hands, moving quickly to get a crumbly dough.

Pour in just enough cold wine to bind the crumbs together and get an even dough. Shape a ball and place it in the fridge for at least an hour, covered in plastic wrap.

Preheat the oven to 350°F. Oil and flour a 10-inch cake pan.

Roll out the dough on a floured work surface and pat into the prepared cake pan, using your fingers so that the dough remains uneven and thick.

Bake the crumbly cake until it is crunchy and golden. This should take around 40 minutes.

I've replaced the eggs used to bind the dough with wine.
Use a really fruity one, such as an aromatic Traminer or chardonnay.

FLAKY ORANGE CAKE

This is a really easy cake to make, but it requires a lot of attention when you're turning it out. But don't panic if a little sticks to the bottom of the cake pan—just remove it with a spatula and put it back on the cake when it is still hot. If you're in a hurry or you don't want to make it yourself, 100 percent vegan puff pastry is easy to find in supermarkets. This flaky cake is an old passion of mine. I've just changed the recipe a little by adding almonds and replacing the dairy butter with vegan butter.

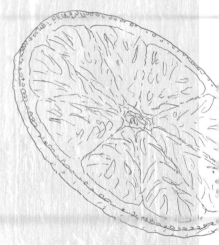

Mix the butter with the brown sugar in a mixing bowl, beating it in with a whisk until they are completely blended, then spread the mixture in a nonstick 10-inch cake pan, sprinkle the almond flakes on top, and refrigerate for half an hour.

Preheat the oven to 400°F.

Cut the unpeeled oranges into fine, horizontal slices, then spread them over the butter base in a single layer, slightly overlapping one another.

Use a rolling pin to roll out the puff pastry on a floured work surface and cut a piece that is slightly bigger than the cake pan, then place it over the oranges and fold the edges toward the bottom of the pan.

Prick the pastry with the tines of a fork to stop it puffing up when baking, then place in the oven and bake until it turns golden brown. This should take around 30 minutes.

Remove from the oven, place the serving plate on top of the cake pan, and turn out the cake with a quick movement, taking care not to burn yourself.

You can also garnish the cake with vegan dark chocolate chips before serving.

4 tablespoons (½ stick)
vegan butter

½ cup light brown sugar

2 tablespoons almond flakes

2 oranges

8 ounces vegan Puff
Pastry (page 22)

Flour, for dusting

FOR 8 PEOPLE

APPETIZERS

Winter Crostini, 150

with Sweet and Sour Carrots

with Leeks in Red Wine Sauce

Grilled Polenta with Radicchio

Soft Polenta with Deep-Fried
Artichokes, 151

Holiday Donuts, 152

Potato and Bean Salad, 154

Robust Salad with Cauliflower
and Olives, 155

Crescenti from Bologna, 156

Blanched Cardoons with
Fragrant Mayonnaise, 157

Sicilian Fritters with Spicy
Catalogna Chicory, 158

FIRST COURSES

Barley Soup, 159

Tuscan Kale with Toasted Bread, 160

Ribollita Soup with Thyme, 162

Mesciua Spezzina/Legume Soup, 163

Pizzoccheri Pasta with Savoy Cabbage
and Borlotti Beans, 164

Rigatoni with Lentil Ragout, 165

Calamarata Pasta with Mushrooms,
Beans, and Greens, 166

Orecchiette with Broccoli Rabe, 168

Flour Gnocchi, 169

Cannelloni with Trevisano Radicchio, 170

Tortelli Pasta with Wild Greens
and Potatoes, 171

WINTER

MAIN COURSES

Garden Boil, 172

Vegetable and Legume Loaf, 174

Cardoons with Béchamel Sauce, 175

Baked Trevisano Radicchio, 176

Milanese "Meatballs" with Cabbage, 177

Stuffed Escarole with Olives,
Pine Nuts, and Raisins, 178

Foil-Baked Vegetables, 179

Marjoram-Stuffed Artichokes, 180

Potato and Celery Stew, 182

Cauliflower Strudel, 183

DESSERTS

Italian-Style Trifle, 184

Fried Apples, 185

Caprese Chocolate Cake, 186

Almond Florentines, 187

Pear Tart, 188

WINTER CROSTINI

We're used to making crostini into little delicacies, but once upon a time they were how people got around throwing away stale bread. Farmers would toast it over the fire and eat it with just a drizzle of oil. Just imagine Tuscan *fettunta*—garlic bread—or the many kinds of bruschetta. My mom also used to do this. When I was little and we still had a wood-burning stove at home, she would give us bread that she had toasted over the fire, dressed with oil and salt. We had recently moved to Florence from the south and she still had her country bumpkin ways, which were held to be a little "exotic" during those times.

CROSTINI WITH SWEET AND SOUR CARROTS

5 carrots

Extra-virgin olive oil

Salt

About 1 teaspoon light brown sugar

2 to 3 tablespoons white vinegar

4 slices seeded vegan whole wheat bread, toasted

Freshly ground black pepper

Chopped fresh chives

Thinly slice the carrots with a vegetable slicer. Heat a little oil in a medium skillet. Sauté the carrots over high heat. Move the pan often so that the carrots don't stick to the bottom and cook them until they are caramelized, about 10 minutes. Season with salt, then add the brown sugar and vinegar, tasting to see whether the level of sweet and sour is to your liking. Cook for another minute, then arrange the carrots on the toast and sprinkle with pepper and chives.

CROSTINI WITH LEEKS IN RED WINE SAUCE

2 large leeks

Extra-virgin olive oil

Salt and freshly ground black pepper

½ cup red wine

4 slices vegan white bread, toasted

Cut the leeks, including part of the green tops, into rounds that are not overly thin. Heat a little oil in a medium skillet. Sauté the leeks, with salt and pepper to taste. Stir often so that they fry lightly without changing color. When they are almost cooked—you'll see that they are almost translucent—pour in the wine and continue to cook until they start to look almost creamy. This should take around 15 minutes—you can add a few tablespoons of water if necessary. Arrange the leeks on the toast and top with a sprinkle of pepper.

GRILLED POLENTA WITH RADICCHIO

2 heads Trevisano or red radicchio (better if late variety)

Extra-virgin olive oil

1 shallot, sliced

Salt

4 slices polenta

1 sprig flat-leaf parsley, chopped

Freshly ground black pepper

Cut the radicchio into thin strips. Heat a little oil in a large skillet. Sauté the radicchio, together with the shallot. Season with salt, then leave it to cook, stirring often, until the radicchio turns soft and browned, but still crisp. This should take around 10 minutes. Grill the polenta or roast in the oven at its hottest setting, then arrange the radicchio with the parsley and a sprinkling of pepper on top.

SOFT POLENTA
WITH DEEP-FRIED ARTICHOKES

I wanted to hark back to the tradition of Venetian polenta. I've removed the salted codfish, for obvious reasons, and I've added the artichokes—vegetables with tons of flavor and great texture on the palate—with Venetian castraure artichokes in mind, a purple kind of artichoke that are the specialty of Sant'Erasmo, a small island in the Venetian lagoon. The castraure are the top part of the artichoke plant, which are cut straight away to allow the so-called *botoli*—the side shoots—to grow. In Rome, the first artichokes are called *cimaroli* and are ready in February. They are extremely tender and flavorful, and are great fried.

Clean the artichokes, removing and discarding the toughest leaves and tough part of the stem, and cutting off and reserving the most tender part of the stem. Quarter them and submerge them in a bowl of water with some lemon juice, so that they don't blacken.

Pour the flour into a bowl and add the cold sparkling water, stirring constantly with a whisk to prevent lumps from forming, until you get an even batter, then leave it to rest in the refrigerator for around an hour.

Chop the tender artichoke stems which you have set aside. Heat 2 tablespoons of olive oil in a large skillet, then add the artichoke stems, garlic, some of the marjoram, and an inch of water. Season with salt and cook until they are tender and a nice sauce has formed. Remove the garlic.

Bring the remaining water plus more salt to a boil, then sprinkle in the cornmeal or polenta, stirring with a wooden spoon. Cook for another 25 minutes. The polenta should turn out rather soft.

Add the artichoke sauce to the polenta and stir well. Heat a generous amount of peanut oil in a large, deep skillet. Toss the artichoke slices in the batter and fry them in the oil until golden.

Divide the polenta among four bowls, add the fried artichokes, and garnish with a few leaves of marjoram and a sprinkling of pepper.

4 purple artichokes
Juice of 1 lemon
1⅔ cups all-purpose flour
About ¾ cup sparkling water, chilled
Extra-virgin olive oil
1 garlic clove
Leaves from 1 sprig marjoram
Around 5 cups water
Salt
2 cups cornmeal or polenta
Peanut oil, for frying
Freshly ground black pepper

FOR 4 PEOPLE

Try replacing half the cornmeal with chickpea flour: It goes great with artichokes.

HOLIDAY DONUTS

Since they had to be ready for Christmas Eve, my grandmother would make the dough on December 23 and go to bed. Then she would get up to fry them in a 5-quart cast-iron skillet filled with oil over the fire in the fireplace. She would fry enough to fill a whole basket, because they had to last for the entire holiday season and she always gave loads away. Fried donuts (*i zippuli*, as she called them) that are a few days old are scrumptious when warmed over the fire, so that they burn a little, but everyone in my family loved to eat them even when cold and a little hardened. My Aunt Montagna always said she liked them to be hard enough to give her the hiccups! What follows is the recipe that came about after an exhausting round of calls between her, my mom, and my Aunt Ferdinanda in an attempt to define what my grandmother's original recipe actually was.

FOR AROUND 12 DONUTS

2 cups potatoes (about 1 pound cooked whole)

1 ounce fresh cake yeast (or 3 teaspoons active dry yeast)

About ¾ cup warm water

Salt

About 2½ cups all-purpose flour

Oil, for frying (best if extra-virgin olive oil)

Boil the potatoes, peel them, put them through the potato ricer when still hot, and place them in a large bowl.

Dissolve the yeast in ½ cup of the water and add it to the potatoes, stirring it in, then season with salt. Gradually add the flour to make the dough. The amount of flour will depend on the how much moisture is in the potatoes, so be careful to not add too much. The dough should be a little sticky. If it becomes too hard, soften it with a little warm water. Leave it to rise in a warm place for around 2 hours.

Half-fill a large, deep pan with oil and heat over high heat until it starts to simmer.

Shape the risen dough into 2-inch donuts with slightly oiled hands and submerge them in the hot oil a few at a time. They will float immediately. Don't worry if they're not even. Trust the pan; it will take care of everything. Make sure the donuts are golden on both sides, then remove them with a skimmer and place them on paper towels to dry. Sprinkle some salt on top to finish.

If you are making these for children, roll them in sugar as soon as they come out of the pan.

POTATO AND BEAN SALAD

Here I'm combining two ingredients that, for centuries, have formed the basis of the diet for the poor classes of the entire planet. In some ways, potatoes and beans know no borders. Throughout the whole of Italy, they were a staple food on peasants' tables, because they cost so little and are so nutritious. Today, beans are especially appreciated for their vegetable protein content, which is particularly important in the vegan diet. In my house we often finished up dinner with a salad containing still warm, boiled potatoes, mixed with what was available. During the summer, my grandmother would add tomatoes, fresh chili pepper, and basil. What you have here is the winter version.

Cut the onion into thin rounds and remove some of its bite by putting the pieces in a bowl of salted water or water and vinegar, for around half an hour, then drain well

Combine the onion, potatoes, beans, sun-dried tomatoes, olives, and a generous pinch of oregano in a high-rimmed serving dish. If spicy is your thing, roast the dried chili pepper over a flame, crush it, and add it to the salad.

Season with plenty of oil, salt, and pepper.

Stir well, taking care so the potatoes do not break into pieces.

You could try pureeing two to three sun-dried tomatoes with the oil you are using for the dressing—the salad will be all the more delicious and the oil will turn a lovely red color.

1 sweet red onion

Salted or vinegared water (to soak the onion)

4 large yellow potatoes, boiled, peeled, and diced

1 cup white beans, boiled

A few sun-dried tomatoes in oil

A handful of baked olives

Oregano

Extra-virgin olive oil

1 dried chili pepper (optional)

Salt and freshly ground black pepper

FOR 4 PEOPLE

ROBUST SALAD
WITH CAULIFLOWER AND OLIVES

In Naples, they use this salad to "strengthen" their Christmas Eve dinner, which—according to tradition—has to be light. In actual fact, the dishes that appear on the dinner table come Christmas Eve really have no need of strengthening, as they are rich and extremely nutritious. Tradition, however, dictates that this salad be made without fail and that it should be present throughout the entire holiday period. *Papacelle* are round, fleshy peppers that are typical of the Campania region.

FOR 4 PEOPLE

1 medium cauliflower

*1 small head curly
endive, chopped*

*A handful of Gaeta or similar
black olives, pitted*

*A handful of green
olives, pitted*

*¾ cup pickled vegetables,
drained*

*4 pickled papacelle peppers, if
you can find them, sliced, or
slices of pickled bell peppers*

*A handful of salted capers,
rinsed and drained*

Extra-virgin olive oil

White vinegar

*Salt and freshly ground
black pepper*

Cut the cauliflower into florets and then steam them in a pot until when they are still al dente.

Mix the endives with the olives, pickled vegetables, pickled peppers, and capers in a high-rimmed serving dish.

Add the cauliflower and dress with a generous drizzle of oil, vinegar, and salt and pepper.

Of course I have gotten rid of the traditional salted anchovies, which in no way affects the rich flavor of this salad.

CRESCENTI FROM BOLOGNA

In Bologna, they call these *crescenti*—"crescents"—and, as Pellegrino Artusi said, they are simply "the fried dough that everyone is familiar with and knows how to make, with the only difference being that the Bolognese people add some lard when mixing the flour with chilled water and salt, in order to make it softer and easier to digest." I've replaced the lard with extra-virgin olive oil. In my husband's family anecdotes—he has distant Bolognese origins on his father's side—there was an uncle who, when he was young, would come home at night and say, "I can smell *crescenti*. . . ." And his mother would get out of bed and make *crescenti* that were as light as a cloud in no time at all.

FOR 4 PEOPLE

1 tablespoon active dry yeast

Warm water

2 cups all-purpose flour, plus more for dusting

Pinch of salt

2 tablespoons extra-virgin olive oil

Peanut oil, for frying

Dissolve the yeast in a little warm water. Sift the flour together with the salt into a large bowl, leaving a well in the center. Put the yeast mixture and the olive oil in the middle.

With your hands, start to incorporate the flour with the liquid and add warm water as needed to get a smooth, even dough, then leave it to rise, covered, for around 2 hours.

Roll out the dough with a rolling pin on a floured work surface until it is about 1½ inches thick, then cut it into diamonds that are around 3 inches long along each side.

Fill a deep medium skillet about two-thirds full with the peanut oil and heat over high heat. The oil is ready when it starts to sizzle.

Fry the *crescenti* a few at a time, turning them once only, and removing them from the oil with a skimmer when they have just turned golden. Dry them on paper towels and serve immediately.

Since you need to try these as soon as they are ready, the person doing the frying usually doesn't sit down at the table. Instead they pass the *crescenti* to their guests, who eat them immediately. Some people like to add a tablespoon of white vinegar to the dough so that they turn out drier.

BLANCHED CARDOONS WITH FRAGRANT MAYONNAISE

Cardoons look like celery but taste like artichokes. Their crunchy, substantial texture makes them perfect for extremely elaborate recipes, but they are also delicious boiled and seasoned with just a little olive oil and lemon. Cardoons are tremendously flavorful vegetables, not to mention extremely healthy, thanks to their iron and vitamin C content. In prime position, we have the *cardo gobbo di Nizza Monferrato*—"the hunchbacked cardoon of Nizza Monferrato"—which is the most tender. This cardoon variety really grows with a hunchback—a certain point it is folded on the side and covered with earth, to whiten it which makes it more tender and sweet. That's why cardoons are often simply called *gobbo*—"hunchback"—in Tuscany and Lazio, and cardoons can be made in a million different ways. You can tell they are good quality when they are white and silver.

Buy cardoons that are still tightly closed and a light, silver color. Green cardoons are tough and fibrous and if they are open, it often means they are old.

Remove the outer stalks and cut the others into 2½-inch pieces, then use a sharp knife to remove the outer strands and toss them into a bowl of water with some lemon juice. Boil them in a large pot with a generous amount of salted water, together with the flour and more lemon juice. It will take about an hour for them to become soft yet still crunchy.

Whip the mayonnaise in a bowl with the capers, olive paste, garlic, and a little lemon zest. Be sure to remove the garlic at the end. If the mayonnaise is too firm, dilute it with a little lemon juice. Top it off with some pepper.

Serve the cardoons on a tray with the mayonnaise in a small bowl on the side.

You can also give each guest a bowl of mayonnaise with three or four pieces of cardoon in it.

2 pounds cardoons
Zest and juice of 2 lemons
Salt
1 tablespoon all-purpose flour
1 batch Mayonnaise (page 18)
A handful of capers, rinsed and chopped
1 tablespoon olive paste
½ garlic clove
Freshly ground black pepper

FOR 4 PEOPLE

SICILIAN FRITTERS
WITH SPICY CATALOGNA CHICORY

These fritters, known as *panelle*, come from Palermo, where they have been sold on the street for a thousand years eaten between slices of a typical bread from Palermo—known as a *mafalda*—with sesame seeds on top. "Bread and fritters" is the street food that symbolizes this city. People line up at the fritter maker set up on a street corner or in the busiest squares. The *panelle* are a kind of fritter made with chickpea flour and water—in fact, very similar to fried polenta, yet much tastier. The recipe that I'm giving you here is not a classic pairing, but I promise you that the Catalogna chicory (also known as Italian dandelion), with its slightly bitter and spicy taste, goes wonderfully with these fritters.

FOR 6 TO 8 PEOPLE

4 cups chickpea flour

6 cups cold water

1 bunch flat leaf parsley or wild fennel, chopped

Salt

Peanut oil, for frying

2 pounds Catalogna or other chicory, cut into pieces

Extra-virgin olive oil

1 dried chili pepper

1 garlic clove, crushed

Freshly ground black pepper

Add the chickpea flour to the cold water in a large bowl, a little at a time, beating it in with a whisk to prevent lumps from forming, then add the parsley or fennel. Pour the mixture into a large skillet, season with salt and cook over low heat for 30 to 40 minutes until it is nice and firm, like polenta.

Turn out the mixture and spread it between two layers of parchment paper, until it is around 1 inch thick, then leave to cool.

Cut out 3-inch squares or triangles of the dough. Heat a generous amount of peanut oil in a large, deep skillet over high heat. Fry the pieces of dough until they puff up and turn golden brown.

Blanch the chicory in a large pot with plenty of salted, boiling water, then drain it. Heat a drizzle of olive oil in a large skillet. Sauté the chicory in the oil with the chili pepper and the garlic. Season with salt and black pepper to taste, then remove from the heat when it is thoroughly cooked.

Use the chicory as if it were a sandwich filling between the fritters.

Once upon a time, doughs made with chickpea flour were left to cool in wooden molds that left floral designs on the fritters. The impressions would disappear soon after they were fried, thus the presence of the design on the fritter was an indicator of freshness.

BARLEY SOUP

Gerstuppe, as it is called in Alto Adige, is a frugal yet filling dish. Usually hausfrau make it by adding a slice of speck ham to the vegetables; however the vegan and vegetarian version is also very flavorful and undoubtedly lighter. You can add beans or mushrooms to give it some texture and flavor. I'm really fond of this simple recipe that I learned from a cook in a Val Gardena hotel, where we used to go when we took our children skiing. It will be clear to you straight away that it has been changed a little—the cook in question didn't use extra-virgin olive oil at all. . . .

Clean the vegetables, cut the leek (including the green tops) and the carrot into rounds, and chop the celery, onion, garlic, and parsley.

Heat a little oil in a large pot. Sauté these vegetables in the oil until they are lightly fried, then add the water, bring to a boil, and add the barley.

After the mixture has been cooking over low heat for around 15 minutes, add the potatoes, then season with salt and pepper.

Cover and cook until the barley is tender and the soup is still quite liquid. This should take a further 15 minutes.

A drizzle of oil before serving can never go wrong.

Pearl barley cooks fast, but if you have time, you can use whole-grain or hulled barley, which is less refined than pearl barley and more nutritious. However, both need 12 to 24 hours' soaking time and take a long cooking time.

1 leek

1 carrot

2 celery stalks

1 large onion

1 garlic clove

1 sprig flat-leaf parsley

Extra-virgin olive oil

About 6 cups water

1¼ cups pearl barley

2 potatoes, diced

Salt and freshly ground black pepper

FOR 4 PEOPLE

TUSCAN KALE WITH TOASTED BREAD

I'm going to quote Pellegrino Artusi again, because he's just so funny! On the subject of cabbage with toasted bread, a traditional Florentine soup, he has this to say: "It's a Carthusian dish or a punishment inflicted upon a glutton," and there is no doubt that he was thinking about himself. . . . In actual fact, cavolo nero (also known as Tuscan kale), when simply boiled and layered on bread and dressed with a drizzle of oil along with its own stock, is a real delicacy. I'm giving you a recipe that includes beans, too, which is more similar to a Lombardy soup; however, it was also created in Florence. And, to tell you the truth, I sautéed the vegetables in the pan a little, heeding the advice of Pellegrino and adding a bit of verve that is typical of Southern cuisine.

FOR 4 PEOPLE

2 cups dried white beans (Toscanelli or cannellini)

2 bunches Tuscan kale (around 4 cups)

Extra-virgin olive oil (fresh oil, if possible)

1 garlic clove, unpeeled, plus more to rub bread

Dried chili pepper, finely chopped, to taste (optional)

Salt and freshly ground black pepper

4 slices vegan Tuscan bread, rubbed with garlic and toasted

Soak the beans, covered with water, in a bowl overnight, then drain them into a pot filled with around 2 quarts of water and cook them, covered, over low heat, until they are soft but still whole. The water should just be simmering and it will take around 2 hours.

In the meantime, remove the toughest leaves from the kale, blanch them in a large pot of salted, boiling water, and then remove them with a slotted spoon.

Heat a little oil in a large skillet. Sauté the kale in the oil, together with the garlic, some chili pepper, if you like spice, and season with salt and black pepper to taste. Add the beans with some of their stock, then cook over high heat just long enough for it to develop flavor.

Place a slice of garlic-rubbed toasted bread in each bowl, then add an abundant ladle of kale and beans on top plus a little of the cooking stock.

Drizzle a generous amount of fresh oil on top and serve.

In Florence, we are very demanding when it comes to Tuscan kale. The good, delicate ones are best after the first frost, so we eat them from December onward. Toscanelli beans are perfect, as they have a thin skin and are full of flavor.

RIBOLLITA SOUP WITH THYME

This is the queen of Florentine peasant fare. You'll find it on menus in Florence, but authentic *ribollita* isn't even eaten at home anymore. It used to be leftover vegetable soup, which contained nothing more than cabbage and beans that peasants would boil on the fire in the morning for breakfast. Today it's made to be eaten immediately, or prepared—at the very most—half a day in advance and with lots of different vegetables. The first time I ate it was in Impruneta, at an outdoor refreshment station in a pine forest just outside the town. My father bought us ribollita instead of ice cream for a snack. It was served in little earthenware pots, and for us children it was like a game.

FOR 4 PEOPLE

1 cup dry white beans
  (Toscanelli or cannellini)

Salt

Extra-virgin olive oil

1 garlic clove, chopped

1 onion, diced

1 sprig thyme

2 celery stalks, sliced

1 carrot, sliced

3 cups chopped Tuscan kale

¼ savoy cabbage, chopped

1 bunch Swiss chard, chopped

2 potatoes, diced

½ cup tomatoes, peeled
  and crushed

Freshly ground black pepper

Around 1 pound stale
  vegan rustic bread

The beans should be cooked separately—soak them in a bowl of cold water overnight, then drain them and put them in a pot with around 1 quart of water. Cook them over very low heat until they are soft, about 2 hours, seasoning with salt only when they are almost done cooking, otherwise they will toughen up.

Heat a little oil in a large pot. Sauté the garlic and onion in the oil, adding first the thyme and then the celery, carrot, cabbage, chard, and potatoes. Add the crushed tomatoes and continue to cook to let them develop a deeper flavor for a few minutes, then add the stock from the beans and leave to cook until the vegetables have softened. Now is when you should add the beans, too, then season with salt and pepper to taste.

Cut the bread into thin slices and toss them into the vegetable soup, stirring well. Then set it aside for some time. Reboil the soup until it is piping hot, then serve with a drizzle of oil on top.

It's very trendy at the moment to layer the ribollita, alternating between bread and vegetables, then put it in the oven, for around 20 minutes. Some people even add a layer of red onion rings to top it all off.

MESCIUA SPEZZINA/LEGUME SOUP

The name in the Spezzina dialect—*mesciua*—indicates that it is a mixture of legumes and grains that originated with the La Spezia dock workers who would throw everything into the pot that they were able to grab from the bales of grains they unloaded from the ships. It is an extremely frugal dish, without any seasonings or flavorings, which is why the quality of the legumes is essential for getting a good result. The mesciua is made throughout the entire Lunigiana area. Today it has become fashionable and is very popular with the many people who follow a healthy diet.

Soak the legumes and the spelt separately overnight. Drain them, then cook them separately in a large pot, as they have different cooking times, over low heat in around 6 cups of water per pot, until they are soft. This should take around 2 hours for the cannellini beans and chickpeas, whereas the spelt will only take 30 minutes. Season with salt when they are cooked.

Drain the spelt and combine in a single pot with the legumes, including most of the cooking water from the legumes, so that you get a rather watery soup.

Cook for a further 10 minutes to blend the flavors together, then serve the mesciua piping hot with a generous drizzle of oil and a sprinkling of pepper on top.

I recommend adding chopped fresh marjoram for a little flavor.

1½ cups dried cannellini beans
1½ cups dried chickpeas
1 cup pearled spelt
Salt
Extra-virgin olive oil
Freshly ground black pepper

FOR 4 PEOPLE

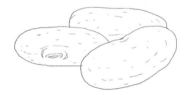

PIZZOCCHERI PASTA WITH SAVOY CABBAGE AND BORLOTTI BEANS

Coming from *piz* ("piece" or "to clamp") real pizzocchero pasta—the certified traditional food product from the Valtellina area, in accordance with the regulations of the Pizzocchero Academy in Teglio—is made without egg, with just buckwheat flour, a small amount of wheat flour, and water. Lately I've been making pizzoccheri pasta often for my vegan friends by removing the butter and cheese and adding borlotti beans instead, which give it texture and substance. You'll see that extra-virgin olive oil goes really well, too.

FOR 4 PEOPLE

For the pizzoccheri

3½ cups buckwheat flour

1 cup all-purpose flour

Salt

About 1 cup cold water

For the sauce

1 small savoy cabbage, cut
    into uneven pieces

1 potato, diced

Extra-virgin olive oil

1 garlic clove

A few sage leaves

1 cup precooked borlotti beans

Salt and freshly ground
    black pepper

To prepare the pasta, sift the two types of flour together with a pinch of salt to form a well on a work surface, adding cold water gradually so as to not add too much, and then knead vigorously until you get an even and elastic dough.

Wrap it in a cloth and leave to rest for around 1 hour, then roll it out with a rolling pin until it is very thin, not more than ⅛-inch thick. Cut 3-inch wide strips from the dough, then cut them again in the other direction, to get a kind of tagliatelle pasta that is about ⅓-inch wide.

To prepare the sauce, submerge the savoy cabbage pieces and the potato cubes in a large pot of salted, boiling water. When the vegetables are almost ready, toss in the pizzoccheri until they finish cooking.

Heat 2 tablespoons of oil in a large skillet. Sauté the garlic and the sage leaves in the oil until the garlic browns slightly. Add the beans, then remove the pizzoccheri and the vegetables with a slotted spoon and toss them into the pan, reserving the cooking liquid.

Season with salt to taste and sauté with the sauce for a few minutes, adding a little of the cooking liquid, so that the pasta is not too dry.

Serve immediately with a sprinkle of pepper.

You could use Swiss chard instead of the savoy cabbage, too.

RIGATONI
WITH LENTIL RAGOUT

The recipe has all the flavor of a good ragout—in this sauce you'll find all the seasonings used in a traditional meat ragout, with a few extra herbs, plus the lentils, which work to add substance and texture for the palate. If the purpose of this sauce was to whet the appetite (from the French, *ragoûter*), I'd say that we have accomplished it—and then some—because this sauce is extremely appetizing and flavorful.

Heat 4 tablespoons of oil in a large skillet over low heat. Add the carrot, celery, onion, and a pinch of salt to the skillet, then sweat the mixture . Keep the heat low as it should cook slowly, without taking on any color.

Just as the vegetables are turning color, add the lentils and bay leaf and let the mixture develop some flavor for a few minutes, then pour in the wine. Leave it to evaporate and then add the tomato sauce, salt and black pepper to taste, and a little chili pepper, if desired.

Leave the sauce cooking, covered, over low heat, until the oil starts to float to the surface. This should take around 30 minutes.

Cook the pasta and drain it when it is al dente, then sauté it in the pan of lentil ragout for a few minutes. Serve the rigatoni with a good sprinkle of roughly chopped parsley on top.

Alternatively, garnish the dish with some chopped celery (including the leaves), parsley, and carrot.

Extra-virgin olive oil

1 carrot, diced

1 celery stalk, diced

1 onion, diced

Salt

1 pound lentils, cooked
and drained well

1 bay leaf

½ cup white wine

2 cups tomato sauce

Freshly ground black pepper

Dried chili pepper, finely
chopped, to taste (optional)

1 pound rigatoni pasta

1 sprig flat-leaf parsley,
roughly chopped

FOR 4 PEOPLE

CALAMARATA PASTA WITH MUSHROOMS, BEANS, AND GREENS

The first few times that I added this pasta to the menu for a few vegan evenings, there was always someone that would look at me suspiciously. I had to constantly explain that it was not fish, but rather a Neapolitan pasta, the shape of which was similar to calamari rings that had been floured and panfried. I have a real passion for calamarata pasta—it's fantastic, has a magnificent texture, and goes perfectly with any sauce. You might also find it fresh at the supermarket and I'm always cooking it with tomatoes and vegetables. It is especially tasty with beans, which slip inside the delicious rings of pasta and become slightly powdery when cooked.

FOR 4 PEOPLE

Extra-virgin olive oil

1 small onion, sliced

1 garlic clove

1 bunch Swiss chard, chopped

Salt

½ pound mixed mushrooms

1 cup cooked cannellini beans

¾ cup tomatoes, peeled and crushed with a fork

Freshly ground black pepper

1 pound calamarata pasta or similarly thick, tubed pasta

Heat 2 to 3 tablespoons of oil in a large skillet. Sauté the onion and garlic clove in the oil.

Add the Swiss chard, season with salt, and leave to fry lightly over a low heat, stirring every so often.

When it is halfway done cooking, add the mushrooms and a little warm water, if needed, then cook covered until the chard and mushrooms are soft—it should take 15 minutes total—then add the beans, too.

Toss in the tomatoes, crushed with a fork, then season with salt and pepper, stir and cook for another 10 minutes.

Cook calamarata pasta, drain it when it is al dente, reserving the cooking liquid, and sauté it with the vegetables for a few minutes, adding a little cooking liquid, if necessary, as it should not be too dry. Serve sprinkled with pepper.

The calamarata is also outstanding with sauce and then baked with breadcrumbs in the oven.

ORECCHIETTE WITH BROCCOLI RABE

This is one of the tastiest examples of regional Italian cooking that is naturally vegan. Orecchiette is truly unique thanks to its shape and robust, rough texture that will hold any sauce. This pasta is emblematic of Apulian cuisine, and the most classic pairing would be with broccoli rabe; however, there are endless recipes that include tomato and other vegetables. If you want to make them at home, you'll need a bit of dexterity: "dragging" the pieces of pasta with the tip of a knife, then wrapping it around your thumb is easier said than done. . . . Today—fortunately—excellent, fresh, homemade orecchiette pasta can be found ready to go, even outside of Apulia.

FOR 4 PEOPLE

2 pounds broccoli rabe

Extra-virgin olive oil

2 garlic cloves, crushed

Dried chili pepper, finely
   chopped, to taste

1 pound fresh orecchiette pasta

Salt and freshly ground
   black pepper

Separate the broccoli rabe tops from the leaves and stems, and chop the stems.

Blanch just the leaves and the stems in a large pot of salted water for a few minutes, then remove them and set aside.

Heat 2 tablespoons of oil in a large skillet. Sauté the garlic cloves and chili pepper in the oil, then add the blanched broccoli rabe.

Bring a large pot of salted water to a boil, then add the uncooked broccoli rabe and the orecchiette.

When they are cooked—the broccoli rabe should be al dente—remove with a slotted spoon, reserving the cooking liquid, and add to the pan of sautéed broccoli rabe.

Sauté it all together for a few minutes, adding salt, a sprinkle of black pepper, and a little cooking liquid, if needed, and serve.

You could also add a drizzle of extra-virgin olive oil at the end.

FLOUR GNOCCHI

My brother-in-law learned to make these from his father, who was from Trieste. He always made these gnocchi on winter evenings, when the family would come together at the end of the week at their seaside home. I had only just met them and I remember that being with him while he cooked helped me to not feel so awkward. Sometimes the gnocchi were a little undercooked— perhaps he'd made them too big—but when dressed with onion that had been sautéed in butter, they were delicious, a real comfort food. I've discovered that there is an eggless version called *passerotti*. I found it in the Trieste cookbook by Maria Stelvio that was published in 1927 for "novices"—newlywed women. She gives a note at the beginning of the book: "The fats given in this book are perfect. However, depending on regional cuisine, you can always use the fat that you prefer." Meaning we have permission to sauté the onion in olive oil instead of butter.

To prepare the gnocchi, sift the flour into a mixing bowl with a pinch of salt and some nutmeg, then add around 1¼ cups of boiling water, with a little salt, beating continually with the whisk, until you get an even dough that is very sticky.

Bring a large pot of salted water to a boil, and then add the dough by the half-tablespoonful, wetting the spoon each time so the gnocchi does not stick. They are cooked when they float to the top. Remove them with a slotted spoon.

Meanwhile, prepare the sauce: Heat a little oil in a large skillet. Sauté the onion with a pinch rosemary and thyme in the oil.

Toss the cooked gnocchi into the sauce. Sauté for a few minutes, just enough for them to take on a bit of color and to absorb the aroma of the herbs. Serve with some pepper sprinkled on top.

When it comes to onion, I never think that adding a few whole sage leaves is a bad thing, as they sauté very nicely.

FOR 4 PEOPLE

For the gnocchi
2½ cups all-purpose flour
Salt
Freshly grated nutmeg
About 1¼ cups boiling water

For the sauce
Extra-virgin olive oil
1 large onion, diced
1 sprig rosemary
1 sprig thyme
Freshly ground black pepper

CANNELLONI
WITH TREVISANO RADICCHIO

Late-variety Trevisano radicchio is the pride and joy of the Treviso region. The technique used to get these oh so tasty and crunchy vegetables is actually very complicated. It was devised by Francesco Van den Borre, who was inspired by the traditional Venetian custom of "whitening" cardoons and celery in containers filled with sand, which helped them lighten. Radicchio is placed in tanks with flowing spring water for two weeks, so that it develops red flowers with a fleshy white stem in the center—this is known as forcing. Then it goes into sand-filled containers in a dark place to take on an even deeper red color and to dry out. Last, it is *tolettato*: cleaned of its rotted leaves to get to the valuable, innermost center. These are not wasted efforts, because the result is an exceptional vegetable.

FOR 4 PEOPLE

1 batch Fresh Pasta (page 22), or ⅓ pound dried durum wheat cannelloni

4 heads late-variety red radicchio (Trevisano if you can find it), thinly sliced

Extra-virgin olive oil

1 sweet red onion, sliced

Salt and freshly ground black pepper

1 batch Béchamel Sauce (page 18)

⅓ cup mixed, toasted almonds and hazelnuts

2 tablespoons vegan bread crumbs

Preheat the oven to 400°F.

Roll the pasta out into a very thin layer, not more than ⅛-inch thick, then cut it into rectangles (at least 16) that are about 4 by 6 inches.

Sweat the radicchio in large skillet with a little oil together with the onion and salt and pepper to taste. Cook, covered, until the radicchio softens, then raise the heat to completely evaporate any liquid. Mix the radicchio in a bowl with a third of the béchamel sauce. Pour a thin layer of béchamel into the bottom of a baking pan.

Place a good dollop of the radicchio filling in the center of each rectangle of pasta and roll them to create the cannelloni, then arrange them, seam side down, on the bottom of the prepared baking pan. If you are using ready-made cannelloni instead, fill them, using a teaspoon, following the same steps.

Mix the almonds and hazelnuts together with the bread crumbs. Cover the cannelloni with the remaining béchamel and sprinkle with the nut mixture, then place in the oven to bake. This should take around 20 minutes.

Try replacing some of the radicchio with pumpkin or winter squash cooked separately in the same way.

TORTELLI PASTA WITH WILD GREENS AND POTATOES

The festival held every year in Luco di Mugello, for two weeks in June, is the most famous tortelli festival out of the many that follow one another in this region during the summer. Potato tortelli, as they are made in Mugello, are delicious because the filling is seasoned with sautéed herbs and vegetables and even tomatoes sometimes. I always recall one of my classmates who would bring to school two slices of bread filled with leftover tortelli as a snack that her grandmother had made the evening before. I was always able to convince her to leave me a bite; it was a real delicacy! I've added some wild greens to contrast and subdue the garlic.

Boil the potatoes, then peel and puree them.

Blanch the wild greens in a pot of boiling water, then squeeze any excess water out and roughly chop them.

Heat a little oil in a large skillet. Brown the garlic clove with the parsley in the oil. Remove the garlic, add the wild greens, and cook for a few minutes to allow them to develop a deeper flavor, then mix them into the potatoes in a large bowl and season with salt.

Roll out the pasta on a floured work surface into a very thin sheet, not more than ⅛-inch thick, then cut out disks about 2½ inches in diameter. Place a heaping teaspoon of filling in the center of each disk, then fold it into a half-moon shape and seal the borders well, pressing down with the back of the tines of a fork.

Clean the skillet and heat 2 tablespoons of oil. Sauté the sage leaves in the oil until they are a bit crisp.

Cook the tortelli in a large pot of salted water, remove them with a slotted spoon, and toss them into the pan of sage.

Sauté them for a few minutes to allow them to take on some flavor, then add the toasted almonds, stir well, and serve.

1½ pounds white potatoes
½ pound wild greens, such as dandelion and borage
Extra-virgin olive oil
1 garlic clove
1 sprig flat-leaf parsley, chopped
Salt
⅔ pound Fresh Pasta (page 22)
Flour, for dusting
5 to 6 sage leaves
⅓ cup toasted almond flakes

FOR 4 PEOPLE

Mushroom sauce is a classic and much loved topping for tortelli.

GARDEN BOIL

4 carrots with their tops

1 medium Romanesco broccoli

1 small cardoon

1 celeriac

4 medium potatoes

2 beets

1 tablespoon all-purpose flour

Lemon wedge

For the yellow sauce

2 tablespoons rustic mustard

2 tablespoons extra-virgin olive oil

For the green sauce

1 sprig flat-leaf parsley

1 tablespoon capers, rinsed and drained

1 tablespoon olives, pitted

½ garlic clove

A piece of green bell pepper

Extra-virgin olive oil

Coarse salt

Freshly ground black pepper

For the red sauce

⅓ cup plus 1 tablespoon tomato sauce

½ onion, diced

1 piece of spicy chili pepper

A pinch of paprika

Salt and freshly ground black pepper

Extra-virgin olive oil

White wine vinegar

Light brown sugar

1 tablespoon cornstarch

A bountiful tray of colorful fresh vegetables, well selected and boiled to perfection, is an ideal main dish on a vegan table. Boiled vegetables can be real delicacies if they are cooked right; they can become bland and fibrous if you overcook them, even by just a few minutes. Here are some simple rules: Prepare everything separately, because the vegetables have different cooking times; boil them in a lot of salted water, so they keep their natural colors; remove them from the water when they are still crunchy, as they keep cooking until they cool.

Cook each type of vegetable separately in salted, boiling water:

After you have cleaned the cardoon thoroughly, add the flour and a lemon wedge to the boiling water so that it keeps its color.

The celeriac can be peeled once cooked; the same goes for the potatoes, but they are nicer to look at when you don't peel them.

To cook the beets more quickly, leave some of the leaf stems attached.

To prepare the yellow sauce, use a whisk to beat the mustard with the oil until you get an emulsion, then put it in a serving bowl.

To prepare the green sauce, place the parsley, capers, olives, garlic, and bell pepper, with salt and pepper to taste, in a blender and blend, adding the oil in a slow, steady stream until you get a nice, even sauce.

To prepare the red sauce, put the tomato sauce, onion, chili pepper, paprika, salt, pepper to taste, and some oil in a small pot. Cook over high heat until it has reduced a lot, then add the brown sugar and vinegar and taste to adjust the sweet or sour level to your liking. Add the cornstarch dissolved in a little water to thicken the sauce, stir, and then remove from the heat.

Serve the boiled vegetables with the three sauces on the side.

VEGETABLE AND LEGUME LOAF

FOR 4 PEOPLE

For the loaf

1 pound white potatoes

Extra-virgin olive oil

4 celery stalks, diced

2 carrots, diced

½ sweet red onion, diced

1 garlic clove, chopped

Salt

1 cup cooked chickpeas

2 tablespoons all-purpose flour

⅓ cup stale vegan bread
    crumbs, plus more
    for dusting

Freshly ground black pepper

Freshly grated nutmeg

1 tablespoon chopped
    rosemary

For the caper sauce

1 tablespoon brined capers,
    rinsed thoroughly

A few sun-dried tomatoes

1 cup Mayonnaise (page 18)

For the paprika sauce

⅔ cup tomato sauce

1 tablespoon extra-
    virgin olive oil

1 tablespoon spicy or
    sweet paprika

A pinch of salt

I just have to quote Pellegrino Artusi again, who is almost obligatory to note when speaking about a loaf. Our dear Pellegrino says, "Mister Loaf, please do come in, do not hesitate. I would like to introduce you to my readers also. I know that you are modest and humble as, given your origins, you know less than many others. However, take heart and do not doubt that with a few words said in your favor that someone will try you." In other words, it was a frugal dish. For me, on the other hand, it's the height of deliciousness, so soft and filled with flavor, just asking to be cut into slices. . . .

Preheat the oven to 350°F.

Boil the potatoes.

Heat a little oil in a medium skillet. Cook the celery, carrots, onion, and garlic in the oil until they soften, and then season with salt.

Mash the potatoes together with the chickpeas in a large bowl, adding the cooked vegetables and the flour, bread crumbs, salt and pepper to taste, a good sprinkle of nutmeg, and rosemary.

Shape the loaf with your hands, roll it through the bread crumbs, wrap it in a lightly oiled sheet of parchment paper, then in aluminum foil, and place on a baking sheet. Bake for around 35 minutes.

To prepare the caper sauce, chop the capers and tomatoes together, then mix them in a bowl with the mayonnaise, diluted with a little water.

To make the paprika sauce, reduce the tomato sauce in a small pan, together with the oil, paprika, and salt, then emulsify it with an immersion blender.

Serve the loaf in slices with the sauces on the side.

If it's better for you, you can turn out the mixture into a parchment-lined bread pan that is then oiled and sprinkled with vegan bread crumbs.

CARDOONS WITH BÉCHAMEL SAUCE

I've already talked about Nizza Monferrato hunchback cardoons, which may be hunchbacked but are also white, tender, and flavorful. These cardoons are the main feature of *bagna cauda*, one of the most traditional recipes from the Piedmont region, but are also great floured and fried, cooked together with tomatoes, fried with garlic, or even grilled. This recipe is for Piedmont-style cardoons with béchamel sauce, one of my favorite recipes. The recipe has been adapted to a vegan diet, and it's still delicious.

Preheat the oven to 400°F.

Clean and prepare the cardoons, then cut them into 3-inch pieces. Cook in a large pot of salted, boiling water with the flour and lemon.

Remove them while they're still crunchy and roll them in flour. Heat some oil in a medium skillet and brown the floured cardoons in the oil until golden.

Put some béchamel sauce in a 9-by-13-inch baking dish, just enough to cover the bottom, before adding the cardoons in layers. Add salt and pepper to taste, then cover with the remaining béchamel.

Dust with bread crumbs and bake for around 25 minutes.

Alba white truffle goes very well with these cardoons— if you're lucky enough to be able to get hold of some that have been ethically sourced, grate a little over this dish.

2 hunchback cardoons

1 tablespoon all-purpose flour, plus more for dusting

½ lemon

Extra-virgin olive oil

2 batches Béchamel Sauce (page 18)

Salt and freshly ground black pepper

2 tablespoons vegan bread crumbs

FOR 4 PEOPLE

BAKED TREVISANO RADICCHIO

For this recipe, use deep red, long radicchio leaves—they're so crunchy with a pleasantly bitter taste. We used them in the last season in a recipe for fettuccine. Late-growing radicchio from Treviso is delicious cooked or raw in a salad—either way, it only needs a drizzle of oil and a pinch of pepper to bring out its best flavors. You can also try grilling it: It's perfect for a mixed grill.

FOR 4 PEOPLE

Extra-virgin olive oil

4 heads late-growing Trevisano or red radicchio

Salt and freshly ground black pepper

Preheat the oven to 350°F. Lightly oil a baking dish.

Cut the radicchio heads in half before laying them out next to each other in the prepared baking dish.

Drizzle on some more olive oil, a touch of salt, and a good pinch of pepper before baking them for around 20 minutes, until the radicchio is cooked but still crunchy and slightly browned.

Serve warm, though it is also delicious at room temperature with an extra splash of olive oil and a little more pepper to taste.

A few drops of traditional balsamic vinegar from Modena goes well with this dish.

MILANESE "MEATBALLS" WITH CABBAGE

In Milan, traditional meatballs are made using leftover meat rolled in bread crumbs and fried in butter. In 2008, the dish got a mark of authenticity from the city's Municipal Authority in the form of the Denominazione Comunale. In local dialect, they're called *mondeghili*, which dates from the period of Spanish rule over the city, coming from the Spanish *albóndiga*, meaning "meatball," which then became *albondeghito*, only to end up as *mondeghilo* in the Milanese dialect. In some restaurants, this dish is served wrapped in savoy cabbage, being confused with another traditional Milanese dish known as *polpett de verz*—"cabbage meatballs," which is also wonderful. I was lucky enough to try this version in a very traditional restaurant, and sticking with tradition here seems right. Of course, some substitutions have to be made, in this case, replacing meat with potatoes, but I like the story of this dish and of how it got its name, so please do enjoy my vegan "meatballs."

Boil the potatoes, then peel and mash them in a large bowl while still hot.

Soak the soft inner part of the bread roll in the vegetable broth and then squeeze the excess broth out. Mix the garlic and parsley with the lemon zest, some grated nutmeg, and the soaked bread. Mix well with the potatoes and then combine with the flour and salt and pepper to taste.

Meanwhile, blanch the cabbage leaves for a few minutes in a pot of salted, boiling water.

With wet hands, shape the potato mixture into balls, roll them in bread crumbs, and carefully wrap them in the blanched cabbage leaves.

Lightly oil a large skillet. Sweat the onion in the skillet before adding the cabbage rolls, seam side down.

Move them around by shaking the pan until their color has changed, before adding a touch of wine (and a splash of water, if needed), before lowering the heat and leaving it to simmer for about 10 minutes.

These faux meatballs are also good at room temperature. If you prefer them in a sauce, add 2 tablespoons of tomato sauce and a little water with the wine.

1 pound potatoes

1 vegan bread roll

½ cup Vegetable Stock (page 17)

¼ garlic clove

1 bunch flat-leaf parsley, chopped

Zest of 1 lemon

Freshly grated nutmeg

2 tablespoons all-purpose flour

Salt and freshly ground black pepper

8 to 10 savoy cabbage leaves

Vegan bread crumbs

Extra-virgin olive oil

1 small onion, diced

4 ounces white wine

FOR 4 PEOPLE

STUFFED ESCAROLE
WITH OLIVES, PINE NUTS, AND RAISINS

Stuffed escarole is a traditional Christmas dish in Naples. There, it is served as a side dish, but they also make a good main dish—flavorful and filling. Use small, soft escarole. Some people blanch the escarole in salted, boiling water before stuffing them, but I think this is a shame because it means you lose a lot of their unique flavor. Putting them straight in the pan instead means the escarole cooks with the liquid it releases, giving the dish a more intense flavor.

FOR 4 PEOPLE

⅔ cup pine nuts

⅔ cup raisins, soaked
    and drained

A handful of pitted
    olives, chopped

4 small heads escarole,
    left whole

2 garlic cloves, 1 chopped,
    the other left whole

Salt and freshly ground
    black pepper

Extra-virgin olive oil

Wash the escarole, keeping the four heads intact.

Mix the pine nuts, raisins, and olives in a small bowl. Stuff this mixture between the leaves of the escarole, along with the chopped garlic, some salt and pepper, and a drizzle of olive oil.

Close the escarole with kitchen string. Heat a little oil in a large skillet and add the escarole along with the clove of garlic.

Cook the escarole for around 10 minutes, giving the pan a shake every now and again and adding a little hot water, if needed.

This escarole dish is also delicious cold.
Now and again I add some bread crumbs from leftover bread to the stuffing.

FOIL-BAKED VEGETABLES

Foil baking is a quick and easy way to cook, with the advantages of both baking and steaming your vegetables. It lets you hold in the flavors and aromas of your food, or even concentrate them and make them stronger. There's no specific recipe for this dish—just choose the best seasonal vegetables, wrap them in foil, and throw them in the oven. You'll always get a tasty dish, and it can vary depending on the flavors you choose to add. Herbs are a great resource—simply choosing the right ones lets you spice up even the most everyday dishes.

Preheat the oven to 350°F. Place a sheet of lightly oiled foil in a large ovenproof dish.

Arrange the cauliflower, carrots, potatoes, fennel, and leeks in the prepared dish. Try to keep everything in one layer so the vegetables will cook more quickly and evenly.

Scatter with the sun-dried tomatoes, herbs, and salt and pepper to taste.

Drizzle the vegetables with some olive oil, then form a packet by adding another sheet of foil and folding the edges together tightly to seal well.

Bake for around 30 minutes before serving—keep the packet sealed until it's on the table.

You can also make individual packets.
It goes without saying that a sprinkle of chopped chili pepper would also go well here.

Extra-virgin olive oil
1 small cauliflower, chopped into small florets
4 carrots, julienned
2 potatoes, sliced
2 fennel bulbs, quartered lengthwise
2 small leeks, quartered lengthwise and including some green tops
10 sun-dried tomatoes, soaked briefly in water
Sage, chopped
Rosemary, chopped
Marjoram, chopped
Salt and freshly ground black pepper

FOR 4 PEOPLE

MARJORAM-STUFFED ARTICHOKES

Prepping artichokes takes time and patience—I recommend wearing gloves to prevent staining your hands. Peel off the outer leaves, then cut off the tips, trim the base, slice the artichoke in two lengthwise, and remove any fuzz from inside. Otherwise, if cooking them whole, pull the leaves outward. Throw them in some water with lemon juice to stop them from turning brown, and they're ready to cook. I was always taught to trim the artichokes as little as possible, so as not to waste anything—we only threw away a few leaves and we didn't cut away the entire tip of the leaves, only the pointed end. I remember eating leaf after leaf of artichoke, pulling the hard ones between my teeth to get as much flesh as I could and leaving behind only the bits that really couldn't be eaten and had to be thrown away.

FOR 4 PEOPLE

4 artichokes

Salt

⅔ cup soaked vegan bread crumbs

1 bunch flat-leaf parsley

1 bunch marjoram

1 garlic clove

Extra-virgin olive oil

Freshly ground black pepper

Once the artichokes have been prepped without slicing them in two (see headnote), separate the leaves by gently pushing them outward before lightly salting them.

Combine the bread crumbs, herbs, and garlic in a small bowl along with a drop of olive oil and some salt and pepper. Stuff this mixture between the layers of artichoke leaves before arranging the artichokes upright in a large pot, as close together as possible.

Drizzle on some more olive oil and a sprinkle of salt and a pinch of pepper, then add a splash of warm water to the pan and cook, covered, over low heat until soft, around 30 minutes.

To reduce the cooking time, cut the artichokes in half (see headnote) and then add the stuffing to the center of each half.

POTATO AND CELERY STEW

I looked through all my recipe books and I think this might be the only regional recipe of its kind not to include meat. This recipe comes from the region of Abruzzo. It uses large, thick stalks of celery, cooked slowly with potatoes and very little liquid in a tightly covered pot (if you have a clay pot, all the better). The vegetables become soft gradually, locking in their flavors. It's a simple recipe, but a delicious one nonetheless—the perfect main dish. I really love reheating vegetable stew the next day with a splash of olive oil—sometimes I even eat it cold. I tried that with this recipe, and believe me, if you can resist eating all of it right away, it's even better the next day!

FOR 4 PEOPLE

Extra-virgin olive oil

1 sweet red onion, sliced

2 pounds potatoes, peeled and diced

2 pounds celery, destringed and diced into 1-inch pieces

Dried chili pepper, finely chopped, to taste

Salt and freshly ground black pepper

Heat a little oil in a large skillet. Sauté the onion in the oil.

Add the potatoes and celery.

Let these develop some flavor for a few minutes, giving the pan a shake every now and again, before adding the chili, salt to taste, a pinch of black pepper, and a splash of warm water.

Leave the stew to cook, covered, over low heat until the vegetables are soft. This should take around half an hour.

In the dialect of Abruzzo, celery is called *sellare*—almost the same as English!

CAULIFLOWER STRUDEL

The fine pastry that these vegetables are wrapped in is also used in Trentino and South Tyrol for their classic apple strudel recipe, which is the cousin of baklava—that's why I'm calling this recipe Cauliflower Strudel. In Trieste, they have a similar strudel called *strucolo in strassa*, which is a strudel made from potato pastry filled with fried spinach and then boiled wrapped in a cloth—it's wonderful. This dish is outstanding and makes a perfect main dish.

Preheat the oven to 350°F. Line a baking sheet with parchment paper.

To prepare the pastry, sift the flour and a pinch of salt together in a bowl and make an even dough with the water and oil. Knead the dough vigorously, occasionally dropping it onto a floured work surface, before wrapping it in a cotton cloth and leaving it to rest for an hour or so, under a heated pot.

To prepare the filling, heat a little oil in a medium skillet. Fry the cauliflower in the oil along with the garlic and rosemary. Add salt and pepper and cook uncovered for about 10 minutes. Remove the garlic.

Toast the bread crumbs in a small pan with a little oil.

Cover your work surface with a well-floured cotton cloth. Roll out the dough on this using a rolling pin at first, then flour your hands, make them into fists, and slide them under the rolled dough. Stretch the dough out by gently pulling your fists outward from the center from underneath, until you get a very thin layer of dough.

Oil the dough and sprinkle the toasted bread crumbs over the half closest to you before adding the cauliflower and some more bread crumbs. Use the cloth to help you roll the pastry onto itself and seal the edges well. It will be 14 to 16 inches long. Use a brush to oil the strudel, transfer it to the prepared baking sheet, and bake until it has a nice biscuit color, around 40 minutes. Leave to cool a little before slicing, otherwise the pastry will fall apart.

For the pastry

2 cups all-purpose flour, plus more for kneading

Salt

⅓ cup plus 1 tablespoon warm water

2 tablespoons extra-virgin olive oil

For the filling

Extra-virgin olive oil

1 small cauliflower, broken into florets

1 garlic clove

Leaves from 1 sprig rosemary

Salt and freshly ground black pepper

2 tablespoons vegan bread crumbs

FOR 4 PEOPLE

ITALIAN-STYLE TRIFLE

My mom used to make this all the time and I really didn't like it because of the taste of the alcohol—she used the dregs of liqueurs to soak the sponge cake. Not many people used Alchermes—a lot of women did what my mom did when she made this cake and used it to empty out bottles. But the beautiful red color showing through the serving cups, and the flavors of the spices that are part of the secret, original Alchermes recipe—made by Florentine monks in Santa Maria Novella—are really essential to any Italian-style trifle worthy of the name. The custard is also important (and I did enjoy that growing up)—it should be light and lemony.

FOR 8 PEOPLE

1 batch Custard (page 24)

1 Sponge Cake (page 23)

1 cup Alchermes liqueur
   (or Marashino, Framboise,
   or a spicy liqueur with
   red food coloring)

1 cup vegan chocolate shavings
   (70% cacao with 46% fat),
   plus more for garnish

¾ cup vegan cream,
   for whipping

½ cup powdered sugar

Start with a nice glass serving dish into which the dessert will go, so you can see all the differently colored layers.

After spreading a dollop of custard on the bottom of the glass dish, cut the sponge cake into ½-inch strips, and use some of these to make the first layer.

Mix equal quantities of Alchermes and water, and use a pastry brush to spread a generous amount on the sponge cake to soak in.

Add a generous layer of custard and sprinkle with some of the chocolate shavings. Continue this way, alternating ingredients until the dish is full, reserving some chocolate shavings for garnish.

Finish the dessert by adding a layer of whipped cream, a little powdered sugar, and decorate it with additional chocolate shavings.

For a less sweet sponge cake, add a few tablespoons of a good cane rum.
When strawberries are in season you can also add a few between the layers
to make the dessert sweeter and more traditionally English.

FRIED APPLES

Not fritters! Because, to be precise, a fritter is a kind of rich batter, a mixture of flour and fruit or other things. These apples, on the other hand, are simply sliced and dipped in the batter one by one, just like any other fried food. The batter is the most important thing: It should be light and fragrant; it should puff up slightly while frying and not absorb the oil. So, fry a few pieces at a time in a generous amount of oil and watch out for the smoking point, which is a sign that the oil is no longer usable. I begin frying when the oil starts to bubble, or I drop a little bit of the batter in and if it immediately floats up to the surface and sizzles, I know that the oil is ready.

Combine the flour with the sparkling water in a large bowl, along with the sugar and a pinch of salt. Add the olive oil and lemon zest, then beat until you have a batter that is smooth and rather dense. Cover with plastic wrap and let it rest in the refrigerator for about an hour.

Peel the apples, remove the core, and cut into very thin slices, then wet with lemon juice—otherwise they will turn brown.

Heat plenty of peanut oil in a deep skillet until hot.

Dip the apples into the batter, then fry a few at a time in the oil until they turn a nice golden color.

Remove them with a skimmer and place them on paper towels to drain any excess oil.

Serve hot and sprinkle with sugar.

Sometimes I serve them with some good vegan vanilla ice cream.
Why not also try putting a pinch of cinnamon in the batter; it goes great.

1⅔ cups all-purpose flour, sifted

¾ cup sparkling water

1 scant tablespoon sugar

Salt

1 tablespoon extra-virgin olive oil

Zest and juice of 1 lemon

3 Russet or Golden Delicious apples

Peanut oil, for frying

FOR 8 PEOPLE

CAPRESE CHOCOLATE CAKE

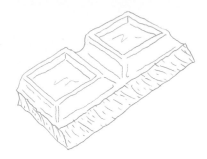

This is the same old story of many other specialties that were created out of some chef's mistake. Tradition has it that this legendary chocolate cake was invented in Capri in the 1920s by Chef Carmine Di Fiore, who forgot to put flour in a cake that he was preparing—for three henchmen of Al Capone, no less! Either way, this cake is very special, because it is soft inside and delightfully crunchy on the outside. I prepare it often for my parents, sometimes varying the ingredients and amounts, and the result is always amazing. Having to remove the eggs, I added cornstarch to help bind it and a little baking powder to replace the egg whites.

FOR 4 PEOPLE

½ cup vegan butter, plus more for pan

Flour, for pan

1⅓ cups blanched almonds

⅓ cup sugar

1½ cups chopped vegan chocolate (70% cacao with 46% fat)

¼ cup almond milk

1 tablespoon cornstarch

1 teaspoon baking powder

Preheat the oven to 350°F. Lightly butter and flour a 10-inch cake pan.

Blend the almonds together with the sugar in a food processor until they are coarsely chopped.

Place the chocolate in the top of a double boiler, along with the almond milk and butter, and melt it, making sure to never let the water boil: steam turns it grainy.

Add the almond mixture, cornstarch, and baking powder last to the melted chocolate and mix until all the ingredients are amalgamated.

Spread the dough evenly in the prepared cake pan, then bake until it forms a light crust on the surface. This will take about 45 minutes.

Let the cake cool before turning it out.

Sometimes I use hazelnuts instead of almonds.
You can also sprinkle a nice dusting of powdered sugar before serving.

ALMOND FLORENTINES

The name can be misleading, as these crispy Almond Florentines are not even Florentine. In fact, they seem to be Tyrolean Christmas desserts, which are not even really Italian at all. I wanted to include them in the cookbook anyway, because they are an example of classic patisserie, even refined patisserie, which requires a minimum of technical capacity and attention and are very easy to prepare. With these Almond Florentines, you'll learn many techniques: how to caramelize the sugar, how to melt chocolate, and how to do a little decoration too.

Preheat the oven to 325°F. Line a baking sheet with parchment paper.

Mix the sugar, cream, and butter together in a deep, heavy-bottomed pot. Boil for 5 minutes, until the sugar has completely dissolved. Remove from the heat and add the almond flakes and orange peel.

Pour the mixture onto the prepared baking sheet and roll it out into a very thin layer.

Once it solidifies, score it with a spatula into squares 1½ inches across.

Place the squares into silicone molds designed for round cookies and bake until they are golden and have spread out in the mold; it will take about 15 minutes. Remove from the oven and allow to cool in the pan. Turn out the Florentines when they are cold.

Melt the chocolate in the top of a double boiler. Spread the bottoms of the Florentines with the melted chocolate and allow them to dry upside down.

Spread a second layer of chocolate over the first and create a wave pattern over the chocolate with the tines of a fork while it is still melted, and allow to dry again.

1 cup sugar
⅓ cup vegan cream for whipping
½ cup vegan butter
3 cups toasted almond flakes
3 to 4 strips candied orange peel, chopped
3 cups vegan couverture chocolate (70% cacao with 46% fat)

FOR 4 PEOPLE

Cut the chocolate into small chunks with a knife before melting in the double boiler.
Couverture chocolate has a high cocoa butter content, which makes it glossy and easy to melt.

PEAR TART

This dough is improperly called short crust pastry, as it has no egg yolks: It is actually a piecrust made with sunflower oil butter instead of regular butter. It is very flaky and, if you don't add sugar, it can also be used for savory pies and quiches. Like the short crust pastry, under no circumstances should it be allowed to get warm when being worked. Therefore, you should knead it quickly, using your fingertips, and use iced water to help bring together the butter and flour. I've developed an unhealthy passion for pepper on cooked fruit. In my opinion, it works great here, but you can omit it if it seems too exotic: The pear tart will taste great anyway.

FOR 4 PEOPLE

1 batch Piecrust (page 23)

3 Bosc pears (or similar)

Flour, for dusting

2 tablespoons light
  brown sugar

Orange zest

Freshly ground black
  pepper (optional)

Wrap the prepared piecrust dough in plastic wrap and allow it to rest in the refrigerator for at least an hour.

Preheat the oven to 350°F.

When ready to bake, cut the pears in half lengthwise without peeling them, core them, then cut them into very thin slices. It will be easier if you place the pear halves flat on a work surface and firmly hold the two sides between your thumb and index finger, so that the slices stay intact while they are being cut.

Roll out the piecrust on a floured work surface and place in a rectangular tart mold (the one I used was 14-by-4 inches, with a removable bottom), then pinch the edges of the dough with your fingers to create a kind of decoration and pierce the bottom with the tines of a fork.

Arrange the pear slices on the pastry, laying them down so that they overlap slightly, almost forming a fan shape.

Sprinkle with brown sugar and a bit of orange zest. Finish off with a sprinkling of pepper (if you like the taste) and bake until the pears take on a pretty caramelized color. This should take around 35 minutes.

Sometimes, I replace ½ cup of the flour for the piecrust with the same amount of finely ground almonds.

INDEX OF BASIC RECIPES

INDEX OF MAIN INGREDIENTS

The recipes marked with a [p] include a photograph.

31901060814805